**Practical Pre-School**

# Special Educational Needs in Practice

## Contents

Illustrated by Cathy Hughes

Published by Step Forward Publishing Limited, Cross Street, Leamington Spa CV32 4PX
Tel: 01926 420046    www.practicalpreschool.com    Published in Great Britain © Step Forward Publishing Limited 2002

Special Educational Needs in Practice  ISBN 1 902438 78 7    All material previously published in *Practical Pre-School*.

# The role of the SENCO: an introduction

The updated Special Educational Needs Code of Practice sets a requirement for all early years settings, including approved childminding networks, to either employ a member of staff or train an existing one as special educational needs coordinator (SENCO). Whilst the organisation of this role may differ among settings, it is a mandatory and very important role with major implications for all areas of early years provision.

The overall responsibility of the SENCO is in monitoring and coordinating the implementation of the Code of Practice within the setting, so if you have just been employed or appointed as SENCO, what is expected of you and who can you turn to for advice? The following headings provide a summary of the areas you will need to give consideration to first of all.

## The Code of Practice and policy for special educational needs

The first thing you will need to do is make sure you are familiar with both the Code of Practice and your setting's special educational needs policy.

The new Code lays down a statutory obligation to ensure that an up-to-date SEN policy is implemented in the running of each group, and you will be responsible for overseeing the operation of this policy. Assuming this policy is appropriate, you will need to make sure that all staff members are aware of the policy and what is expected of them, that it is being carried out and review progress.

You may need to organise a staff training session to explain the policy further and check understanding amongst the staff team. With support from the staff you work with, you will then be in a position to assess how the policy is actually being implemented.

## Coordination of provision for children with special educational needs

Whilst staff working directly with individual children with special needs will be supporting them and observing and assessing their progress, you should support them in making assessments of need and ensure all known information is collected from a variety of sources. This may involve liaison with outside agencies, including those already involved with the child, and will always involve liaison with the parents. You will need to make sure that parents understand your involvement and arrange and attend termly review meetings with everyone involved with the child.

It is important that staff understand they are required to keep records of children's progress, noting concerns, and these will provide valuable information when you liaise with staff to produce Individual Education Plans (IEPs) and plan relevant provision for the child.

## Support for individual children and their families

You will need to work closely with the child's early years worker and parents to decide upon the action to be taken and to plan relevant teaching strategies. It is important that you provide information to parents on the advice and services offered by your local education authority and Early Years Development and Childcare Partnership (EYDCP).

## In-service training and information

As SENCO, you will be expected to provide relevant training for your staff team. This does not, however, need to be delivered solely by you. Early Years Development and Childcare Partnerships play an important part in supporting and training both SENCOs and early years staff, providing opportunities for individuals to develop skills and knowledge, helping them to provide support to staff in assessing and providing for children with special educational needs.

A substantial sum of money has been set aside for SEN training until 2004. A percentage of this has been forwarded to local authorities to provide training for setting-based SENCOs, in particular in the key elements of Code of Practice awareness and special educational needs policies.

Funding should also be available to help partnerships in training and providing area SENCOs who will offer support and guidance to setting SENCOs - so you will not be alone!

## Additional support for the SENCO

Do not feel you should know everything immediately! It will be useful to draw up lists of relevant local and national contacts. Some local authorities compile their own SEN directories.

Contact experts for advice, or to provide staff training and make sure you go to all relevant training sessions.

The role of the SENCO is an important, demanding one, requiring commitment and a willingness to train and to be trained. You will probably have been chosen because of your interest and enthusiasm for the role, probably coupled with previous experiences and understanding of children with special educational needs. Through this challenging role, you will be able to pass on your knowledge and understanding to others and provide a greatly enhanced service to children with special educational needs and their families.

Sue Fisher, early years training consultant.

*'The role of the SENCO is an important, demanding one, requiring commitment and a willingness to train and to be trained.'*

# Check-list for newly-appointed SENCOS

## Familiarise yourself with:

☐ The Code of Practice

☐ Your setting's SEN policy

☐ Your setting's record-keeping systems

☐ Review your setting's system for assessment of individual children's progress and attainment

☐ Establish initial contact with your local Early Years Development and Childcare Partnership to identify training available

☐ Familiarise yourself with local facilities and support services

☐ Organise initial training for staff to ensure they become familiar with the SEN policy and the Code of Practice

☐ Assess resources available for children with special educational needs

### National contacts

**National Association for Special Educational Needs (NASEN)**
Tel: 01827 311500   www.nasen.org.uk

**Council for Disabled Children**
Tel: 020 7843 1900

**National Portage Association**
Contact their administrator on 01935 471641
www.portage.org.uk

**Kidsactive** (formerly HAPA)
Tel: 020 7736 4443   www.kidsactive.org.uk

### Local contact numbers
EYDCP:

Educational psychologist:

Local children's centre:

Local Portage worker:

# The revised
# SEN Code of Practice

The revised SEN Code of Practice came into force in January 2002. There are several changes which all early years professionals and childcare workers need to be familiar with.

One of the most important is the inclusion of children in all early years provision - formal educational settings, private establishments and approved networks of childminders. Previously, only state provision had to have regard to the code.

Every establishment now has to nominate a member of staff as a special educational needs coordinator (SENCO) who will be responsible for monitoring and coordinating the implementation of the Code within the setting. The SENCO will need to be familiar with SEN legislation, the Code of Practice and the facilities and support services available within the local area. Where possible, the SENCO should be trained in identifying and managing special needs.

The new Code of Practice lays a much stronger emphasis on the involvement of the child in the decision-making process regarding their educational future, even at the Foundation Stage. This is an acknowledgement that children have a right to have their voices heard, and their deeper involvement, together with that of their parents, goes some way to ensuring this. Parents will also have new rights of appeal against decisions made by the authorities regarding their child's educational provision.

The Code also provides for a reduction of the paperwork involved in its implementation. Individual Education Plans (IEPs) will focus only on what is additional to and different from the rest of the curriculum. Previously, they were written in full, even when the child was following the same curriculum as his peers. It is assumed that a child's special educational needs fall within a number of broad areas, including communication and interaction, cognition and learning, behavioural, emotional and social development, and sensory and/or physical difficulties. The Code recognises that a child's difficulties could be in two or more

of these areas. It sets out a two-stage model of action and intervention: Early Years Action and Early Years Action Plus.

## Early Years Action

The main signs that suggest a child is having difficulties are that he:

■ makes little or no progress, even when you have used approaches that targeted his difficulties;

■ continues to work at a level well below that expected of a child of his age, in certain areas;

■ displays persistent emotional and/or behavioural difficulties despite behavioural management strategies you may have used;

■ has sensory or physical problems and makes little or no progress despite having personal aids or equipment to support him;

■ has communication and/or interaction difficulties and needs specific support in order to learn.

### What to do:

As SENCO, you should discuss your role with the child's parents and find out as much as you can about the child's difficulties, such as baseline assessments or test results. Ask his parents about any health or physical problems, observe his behaviour and performance and record as much about these as possible.

You should liaise with the child's parents and the child to plan and implement an IEP. Even very young children should be actively involved at an appropriate level in discussions about their IEPs, and be encouraged to share in the recording and monitoring of their progress.

Make sure that the IEP focuses on a maximum of three or four targets and records only strategies that are additional to or different from the normal differentiated curriculum.

Make sure that the child's parents are aware of the local education authority's Parent Partnership Service, collect all known information about the child, together with any new, relevant information from the parents and liaise with outside agents, such as social services, that may already be involved with the child, and collect any relevant information from them. You should also liaise with the educational psychologist (EP) and make sure that support and advice from the Child Psychology Service are given to both parents and colleagues. You will need to work with fellow practitioners and the child's parents to decide on the action to be taken, and to plan teaching strategies. Following this, you should arrange a termly review meeting, involving everybody who has been working with the child.

## Early Years Action Plus

Early Years Action Plus is the point at which you need to involve outside agents who can support and help with advice on new IEPs, provide more specialist assessment, suggest new strategies and possibly offer specialist support or activities. The main signs that will suggest the need to seek more specialised help are that the child:

■ continues to make little or no progress in specific areas over a long period of time;

■ continues to work at an early years curriculum well below that of his peers;

■ continues to experience emotional and/or behavioural difficulties that impede his own learning or that of the group, despite having an individualised behaviour management programme;

■ has sensory or physical needs, requires specialist equipment and/or requires regular support or advice from specialist practitioners;

■ continues to have communication and interaction difficulties that impede the development of social relationships and cause problems with learning.

*'Every establishment now has to nominate a member of staff as a special educational needs coordinator (SENCO) who will be responsible for monitoring and coordinating the implementation of the Code within the setting.'*

**What to do:**

You will need to hold a review meeting with the child's parents to discuss the situation. Collect all the relevant information, such as assessment results, the IEPs and records from other agents such as social workers or medical personnel and liaise closely with the external specialist and the parents to agree on a new IEP, appropriate targets and the teaching strategies to use. It is important to keep regular and careful records – this body of information will prove to be invaluable in the long term in deciding what steps to take next. Set the next review date, making sure that the parents and all the involved agents are invited and involved.

Make sure that the parents are still completely involved with and informed about their child's programme of work and that all relevant records and information are up to date and available for the external specialist to use. You should also liaise with the external agents (including the EP) and make sure their advice and support are made available to both the early years professional and the child's parents. It is important to work with the specialist agent(s), the early years professionals who work with the child, and his parents to decide on a new IEP, the targets, and the teaching strategies. The IEP should be reviewed once per term at a meeting which involves everybody concerned with the child.

Even though each setting's situation is unique, the Code does offer useful ideas of the types of provision and teaching strategies that could be considered. These include any combination of:

- extra adult time to plan and monitor the programmes of intervention;

- provision of different learning materials and equipment;

- individual or group support, or staff development and training to introduce more effective teaching strategies;

- creating small groups within the mainstream setting, which receive extra attention from the practitioner or other adult (for example, teaching assistant, adult helper, other volunteers);

- creating small groups which work outside the teaching room for short periods of time, with a professional or other adult;

- giving the child support out-of-hours, for example at lunch-time or after-school clubs;

- giving the child flexible access within the setting to a base where SEN resources and teaching expertise are available;

- teaching the child in groups which are permanently small and where specialist resources and teaching are available.

**Note:** The Code is written in 'school-based' language, but it nevertheless includes all early years settings.

## Statutory assessment

Parents, maintained schools and nursery schools can ask the LEA to make a statutory assessment of a child. Other early years providers, such as childminders or private nurseries, can bring a child to the attention of the LEA, which then decides whether a statutory assessment is required. The Code stresses the importance of the involvement, at this stage, of the parents of a child who is under five years. The early years provider must supply the LEA with all relevant records, and they must obtain information and advice on health-related matters from the appropriate agents.

When the LEA considers an assessment, it asks what difficulties were identified by the provider, whether individualised teaching strategies were put in place, through Early Years Action and Early Years Action Plus, whether outside advice was obtained regarding the child's

- physical health and function

- communication skills

- perceptual and motor skills

- self-help skills

- social skills

- emotional and behavioural development

- responses to learning experiences

and whether parental views have been considered.

From this evidence, the LEA will decide whether the child should be made the subject of a Statement of Special Educational Needs and the whole process should take no longer than six months. A statement must be reviewed every six months if the child is under five years, or annually if he is older.

It is likely that most children will be beyond early years provision before getting to the stage of needing a statement, but professionals at this level must be aware of the whole process and the new legal obligations.

Collette Drifte is a writer, lecturer, INSET provider and consultant on special educational needs and early years education.

# The Disability Discrimination Act:
## how it affects you

**Disabled children need and want to play as much as and alongside their non-disabled peers. Yet as a result of social and environmental barriers, many disabled children are missing out on this essential part of growing up.**

Play and early years workers are in a position to make a difference, and can begin to lead the way in promoting good practice in inclusive play. Disabled children have a right to play and be included in their local communities. This right is now firmly enshrined in disability legislation.

### The Disability Discrimination Act 1995

The second stage of Part III of the Disability Discrimination Act (DDA), introduced in October 1999, requires service providers to ensure that disabled people (including children) are not discriminated against. Although buildings don't have to be physically accessible to wheelchair users until 2004, when the final phase of the DDA is implemented, everyone is now expected to think about and make 'reasonable adjustments' to the way in which they provide services. This includes providing auxiliary aids and services (such as sign language interpretation or information in Braille) to enable, or make it easier for disabled people to use the service.

Part III of the Act covers all aspects of services to the public including private companies, public sector organisations and voluntary and community groups. In terms of play and recreation services, the Act covers leisure centres, indoor and outdoor playgrounds, play areas in public parks, playgroups and some private nurseries. Although, according to a DfES spokesperson, 'the regulations are very complex and something of a grey area where play and the early years are concerned. As education is exempt from the DDA, any nursery or playgroup, which receives funding from a Local Education Authority, is not currently covered by the

Act. However if a school hall is hired out for "non educational use" to a playgroup or facility then it is covered by the Act'.

It is difficult to say at this stage what the full implications of the legislation will be until cases are brought to court. Nor does the legislation spell out in detail what is meant by 'reasonable adjustments'. However, despite its shortcomings, there is no doubt that the DDA is beginning to raise awareness of disability issues. At the very least a marker has been put down on the principles of equality of access and opportunity; and all play and early years providers (whether or not they are covered by the Act) should be looking towards developing inclusive services which have at their heart a policy of equal opportunities.

Further information on the Disability Discrimination Act can be obtained from the Disability Rights Commission helpline on the following numbers:
Tel: **08457 622633**
Text phone:
**08457 622644**

### Inclusion defined

So what are the main areas that need considering when looking at the development of inclusive early years or play services? The starting point has to include reaching out to parents of disabled children, spending time building up relationships, and listening to what they have to say. It is only through working in partnership with parents, carers and disabled children that good quality inclusive practices can be established.

To be truly inclusive a play environment must address three fundamental components - access, participation and activities - and we will examine each of these in turn. Many supposedly inclusive play environments provide access but fall short on participation. It is no good allowing disabled children to attend if you do not have the appropriate resources to enable them to participate. Making play environments inclusive means that we must examine the types of experiences available to the majority of children and ensure that those experiences are also available to disabled children.

### Access

Clearly physical access for children with mobility difficulties is an issue although the majority of disabled children do not use wheelchairs. In most cases minor alterations can be made which are relatively cheap and can improve physical access. Organisations such as the Centre for Accessible Environments can help in this process. Most pre-school settings can already accommodate pushchairs and so need no adaptations in terms of level entrances. In some cases more permanent physical alterations will be required - such as the provision of suitable toilet facilities.

Access is not just about physical access to buildings but also about ensuring that the needs of visually impaired children are taken into account, and that signs and information is provided in large print and Braille. Colour codes and picture symbols can also be used for children with learning difficulties.

Over and above this, access is about having the will and the commitment to include disabled children. This is far more important than ticking off points on a check-list and declaring your project accessible. Dealing with needs as they arise and making every effort to include and welcome all children is central to this process.

## Participation
Some children will undoubtedly need extra support or help with communication in order to participate - children with challenging behaviour and children with physical disabilities such as cerebral palsy in particular. Children who will not participate or whose behaviour seems inappropriate or obsessive may also need to be encouraged and supported to try out new activities. But you don't need to be an 'expert'. Rather you need practical information from parents such as 'How does the child communicate?' 'What are her likes and dislikes?' 'Does he need any special equipment for feeding?', and so on.

In order for children with speech and language difficulties to participate they need to be able to communicate. There are many methods of communication apart from the spoken language (British Sign Language and Makaton, for example) and it is important for staff and for non-disabled children to be aware, and have some knowledge of these methods. This can be

encouraged by, for example, involving children in games and songs which involve signing - all children seem to love this!

It is also important to provide some training for staff. The charity Kidsactive (formerly HAPA) provides training nationwide on inclusive play and can adapt training packages to suit the needs of early years workers in pre-school settings. There are also a number of organisations offering disability equality training. However, most nursery staff will find that they already have many of the skills needed to work with disabled children, the essential attributes being sensitivity, adaptability and imagination.

## Activities and resources
Play environments must support play experiences that are matched to children's developmental levels and are also individually appropriate. Thus activities and resources must offer a variety of active learning experiences which are geared to the needs of disabled children as well as children from ethnic minorities.

Special play equipment is rarely needed - although some toys for disabled children are useful. Far better to use ordinary toys and equipment with some small adaptations, or toys with sensory stimulation which are naturally inclusive. The RNIB, for example, has a toy catalogue which includes a wonderful range of toys for visually impaired children but which all children can enjoy. The organisation Action for Leisure can advise on all aspects of toys and resources that are appropriate to varying ages as well as disabilities. The other alternative to buying is to borrow - in the UK there are around 1,000 toy and leisure libraries for disabled children run

by Playmatters, the National Association of Toy and Leisure Libraries.

## Challenging discrimination - overcoming barriers
Setting up an inclusive play project is not easy. It presents many challenges, and there are many barriers to overcome - not least barriers of attitude and how society views disability. Negative attitudes from parents and carers of non-disabled children is not uncommon. They may be wary about their own children mixing with disabled children or be ambivalent about the idea of inclusion. Then there are the concerns of parents of disabled children who may worry about the level of care their children will receive, the safety of the environment, and the reactions of other children.

Most of these attitudes arise from fear and ignorance, and it is only through challenging discrimination and awareness raising with parents that we will begin to change attitudes. As for the children, the most common reaction to difference is one of curiosity and acceptance - particularly in the early years. Let's capitalise on this and start the process of moving towards a society where all children, regardless of disability, ethnicity or any other difference, can play together in a supportive environment without fear of prejudice or discrimination.

Rachel Scott, Policy and Publications Officer, Kidsactive.

# Developing your
# SEN policy

The revised Code of Practice places a requirement on all settings in receipt of Government funding to have a written special educational needs policy and a major part of the SENCO's role is the day-to-day operation of this policy.

You may have inherited an existing policy which will need amending to fulfil the requirements of new legislation or you may need to devise a completely new one. Either way, the policy must promote equal opportunities and the inclusion of children with special educational needs and this is an ideal opportunity to analyse your special needs provision and identify what you really want to do.

Guidance on policy is available in the Code of Practice, from your local education authority who will be able to provide details of their policies and procedures and, for non-maintained settings, in the Conditions of Grant.

## Developing the policy
It is important that any policy is understood and followed by all staff members. Involving everyone in its development will help to give a feeling of ownership and increase understanding. This will help ensure that the policy is adhered to and increase sensitivity amongst staff towards children with special educational needs.

The process of developing a policy is as important as the implementation. It offers staff a valuable opportunity to air their views on how they can integrate children with special educational needs.

The policy should reflect the ethos and individuality of your setting and ensure the effectiveness of your practice through inclusion.

## What should it contain?
Before planning your policy, familiarise yourself with all relevant documentation, in particular the Code of Practice and *SEN Toolkit*. Non-maintained settings must also include in their policies the information set out in the Conditions of Grant. You can then use the following headings as

discussion points with staff to ensure thorough and thoughtful coverage.

## Objectives
Discuss what you are hoping to achieve and how it relates to the Code of Practice. This will help you to draw up clear, concise objectives which should reflect the philosophy of your setting.

## Admission arrangements
These should already be in place. What else would you need to consider before admitting a child with special educational needs?

## Identification, assessment and provision for all children with special education needs
The sooner special educational needs are identified, the sooner extra support can be provided. You will need to consider who will carry out assessment of need and how. Think about allocation of resources, including human, and ongoing assessment and review of a child's special educational needs.

## Access to the full Foundation Stage curriculum
Consider differentiation and the levels of support available within your setting for children with special educational needs, including such issues as access for disabled children and how you intend to draw up Individual Education Plans, taking into account the guidance in the Code of Practice for Early Years Action and Early Years Action Plus and for children with statements of special educational needs.

## Partnership with parents
Consider how you inform parents of their own and their child's rights, involve them and take into account their own and their child's wishes and ensure they are aware of the local parent partnership services.

## Links with other relevant bodies
Your policy should include a brief description of your arrangements for

**Useful documents**
*SEN Code of Practice*, DfES 2001
*SEN Toolkit*, DfES 2001
*Requirements of Nursery Education Grant* 2001/2 DfEE

linking with others on special needs issues, exchanging information as necessary. This should include outside agencies and support services. Consider links with schools and other early years settings and in particular transfer arrangements.

## Staff roles and responsibilities
Include brief information on the responsibilities of the SENCO, key workers and other staff members. The name of the SENCO should be in the policy document. Remember to consider arrangements for staff training, in particular SENCO training which should be fed back to the staff team.

You should also look at your arrangements for dealing with complaints about your special educational needs provision, and arrangements for reviewing the policy and addressing problems. These arrangements should take into account the effectiveness of your provision for both individual children and all the children in your setting through assessing the effectiveness of Individual Education Plans, curriculum planning for groups of children and the effectiveness of staff training.

## Reviewing your policy
It is a requirement of the Code of Practice that the policy should be regularly monitored, reviewed and evaluated. No policy should be seen as set in stone. It is important to carry out the review arrangements stated in your policy regularly and be prepared to make changes. Putting your policy into practice will highlight any gaps or problems. Remember, a policy is only as good as its implementation.

Sue Fisher, early years training consultant.

# Existing policies

Newly appointed SENCOs should find that their setting already has a special needs policy. In this situation, it is good practice to conduct an audit. A good starting point would be to assess the success of your existing policy in terms of supporting the children with special educational needs in your setting. All staff members should be involved in this. Assess how effective the policy is in practice by giving thought to the following areas:

### The effectiveness of the systems in place for admission of all children, including those with special educational needs

### The systems in place for the identification of special educational needs

■ How accurate are these?

■ Are staff confident and aware?

### Current provision for children with special educational needs

■ How effective are the Individual Education Plans in supporting children?

■ Is the graduated approach being used correctly?

■ Have reviews taken place? If so, have parents and other specialists been consulted/attended?

■ How effective is the curriculum offered and systems of planning for differentiating needs of all children?

### Systems for observation and assessment of attainment and progress for all children

■ Are these used and adapted to support the learning of children with differing needs?

### Relationships with specialists and other agencies

■ What links have been developed and how successful are these in practice?

### Partnership with parents

■ How involved are they and how happy do they seem, both with the service offered and with their child's progress?

### Effectiveness of staff training

■ Have staff attended relevant training? If so, how has this benefited them and the setting?

■ Has knowledge gained been shared to improve understanding and practice?

### Complaints procedure

■ Have any complaints been received about any area of the special educational needs provision? If so, did systems in place support a successful outcome?

If after carrying out this process, you and your staff team are confident that your policy is effective in providing for the needs of children with special educational needs

within your setting, you do not need to produce a new policy. However, you may need to update it to fulfil the requirements of the Code of Practice and to continue the process of monitoring and reviewing.

Sue Fisher, early years training consultant.

# Developing
## inclusive practice

The updated DfES Special Educational Needs Code of Practice states that the provision for children with special educational needs is a matter for everyone involved in each setting. As SENCO, under the overall direction of the head or manager of your setting, you will need to ensure that all staff members recognise and understand their responsibilities towards all the children in their care.

### Why develop inclusive practice?
It is becoming increasingly accepted that inclusion is the right of every child, whether at pre-school or school. This helps to ensure that equal opportunities are provided for all. All children should be given the power of ordinary experiences and have the right to a broad and balanced curriculum.

Children with special needs will benefit from the atmosphere of a happy, stimulating early years setting. Children learn from doing things for each other and observing each other, and all children in the setting will benefit from working and playing with children with special needs.

Children can only be equal if differences are accepted. Therefore, ensuring your provision is inclusive to all children, rather than focusing on specific special needs, is an important starting point.

### Supporting staff
The staff in your setting working with children with special needs will be responsible for their daily care. Some may lack confidence in this, but it is expected that anyone looking after children should be able to manage a wide range of behaviours and needs. Staff members will also be expected to manage extra helpers working with

the children, but at the same time can learn from such support workers who will often have specialist knowledge. Groups belonging to the Pre-school Learning Alliance, for example, may be able to access a support worker through their local branch to provide some one-to-one support. Other specialists, such as Portage workers and educational psychologists, may also be involved in the care of a child and staff will benefit from their experience and advice.

### Action and adaptations
The Code of Practice states that decisions about which actions are appropriate must be made on an individual basis, through careful assessment of the child's difficulties and their need for different approaches. It is vital to work closely with the parents of each child in building up a detailed picture of such needs. This will help you in being prepared to care fully for each child.

*'For true integration, it is important for the children not just to be there, but to be part of it.'*

It is easy to fall into the trap of thinking you are including all children simply by accepting them into your setting, without making any changes. Therefore, as SENCO, a positive approach to inclusion is to identify what difficulties your setting may pose for children with special educational needs rather than looking at the difficulties their attendance may cause you.

It is often not particularly beneficial to provide special activities or equipment. What is more important is that staff use the information they have received from parents and other sources to adjust approaches to suit individual children.

The Code of Practice states that staff should enrich and extend the normal range of teaching strategies for pupils who may need extra help. For true integration, it is important for the children not just to be there, but to be part of it.

Examples could include:

■ **Story time**: one-to-one support for a child who lacks concentration or whose behaviour may deteriorate in a group situation. Props and visual aids for children with hearing difficulties.

■ **Sensory exploration**: This is strongly linked to working with children with special needs but is equally of benefit to all children, especially less confident children and those who find it difficult to express themselves verbally. A range of sensory equipment, both indoors and outdoors (visual, auditory and tactile), will provide valuable learning opportunities for all children.

■ **Adaptations to the physical environment**: This is sometimes as simple as rearranging the furniture. For example, a less cluttered environment assists movement and extending the area of the home corner will provide play opportunities for children with mobility and vision difficulties. It is also important to keep the layout similar each time the child attends.

As SENCO, there are many ways in which you can support inclusive practice in your setting.

It will help you a great deal if all parents are asked to complete an initial assessment of their child's needs and progress to date. It is also useful to know about the impact of different disabilities. If possible, a home visit will give key staff the opportunity to see how the child is cared for and in particular to gain a better understanding of the care needs involved. This information will help you to help staff prepare for the child's entry to the setting. Remember also to focus on each child's strengths and achievements rather than what the child cannot do. This is a method of assessment familiar to all working in the early years and will encourage staff to have high expectations and set suitable targets.

## Support and training

Make sure that staff have access to relevant support, information and training. Close links with your area early years development and childcare partnership are important as special educational needs and inclusion are priorities and they may be offering relevant training and support.

Local schools and other early years settings may also have experiences to share and could be interested in sharing training, ideas and resources.

Staff may worry that they do not have enough specialist knowledge to care effectively for some children. However, with training, advice, information and support this should not be a problem. Although it is your role to support staff, they should be encouraged to seek some information for themselves. You can support them in this by keeping details of useful contacts and addresses of organisations who will be able to provide useful written information. They may also be able to offer advice on how to make your setting more accessible to children with specific disabilities.

### Useful contacts and publications

Centre for Studies on Inclusive Education (CSIE)
Room 2S203 S Block, Frenchay Campus, Coldharbour Lane, Bristol BS16 IQU. Tel: 0117 344 4007
The CSIE offers a variety of free materials as well as details of relevant publications.

National Association for Special Educational Needs (NASEN)
NASEN House, 4/5 Amber Business Village, Amber Close, Amington, Tamworth, Staffs B77 4RP
Tel: 01827 311500

Disabled Living Foundation
380-384 Harrow Road, London W9 2HU
Tel: 0207 289 6111
Helpline: 0845 130 9177
For advice on adaptations and more.

*Inclusion in Pre-school Settings - Support for Children with Special Educational Needs and their Families* (PLA) ISBN 1 873743 22 X
Tel: 0207 8330991
This is a practical, user-friendly publication containing good advice on working with children with a wide variety of special needs.

*Good Practice in Caring for Young Children with Special Needs* by Angela Dare and Margaret O'Donovan (Stanley Thornes) ISBN 0 7487 2871 6.

Bear in mind the differing needs of children when requesting resources. It is not always necessary to have special resources, but sturdy construction and small world equipment, for example, would be suitable for most children.

Overall, remember that inclusion must ensure all children are valued for who they are, and the more flexible the strategies you use, the more likely that children with a wide range of needs will make progress.

*Sue Fisher, early years training consultant.*

# Early identification **and** intervention

Some children will begin pre-school education already having been identified as having a special educational need (SEN) but a number of special needs will be identified for the first time whilst children are attending early years provision, with a significant chance that you or a member of your team (such as a key worker) will be the one who identifies it.

## What is a special educational need?

It is likely you will first be alerted to the possibility of a SEN through observing that a child is not learning or behaving how you would expect for their age. All special needs will fall into one of the categories stated in the new Code of Practice. These are:

- Cognition and learning difficulties
- Behavioural, emotional and social difficulties
- Communication and interaction difficulties
- Sensory and physical difficulties

Occasionally, a child with a mild level of disability will not be seen as having a special educational need if this does not affect their progress.

*'As SENCO, you can support staff in understanding that it is their depth of knowledge of child development that assists more than anything else in the identification of a special need.'*

## Why is early intervention so important?

The Code of Practice stresses the importance of early identification and assessment and places a requirement on early years settings to make sure that suitable provision is made for any child identified as having a SEN. You have a duty to recognise and identify any SEN in your setting and plan what action needs to be taken to help and support each child.

For those working in the private and voluntary sector, the National Standards emphasise the importance of ensuring appropriate action is taken when a child is identified as having special educational needs. Additionally, and pertinent to the care of all children, standard 3 states that children's individual needs should be met.

## How are special educational needs identified?

Many early years workers lack confidence in identifying special needs, yet have a wealth of experience in meeting children's individual needs. Some children will arrive at your setting already having been identified as having a specific special need, but many more will not. Those already diagnosed are likely to have a label attached to their need and whilst this will help you identify what support they need, it is not imperative. What is important is early intervention to ensure the child reaches their full potential. As SENCO, you can support staff in understanding that it is their depth of knowledge of child development that assists more than anything else in the identification of a special need.

If a child is having difficulty, it is possible staff will be alerted to this early after admission. However, it is more likely that concerns will be raised when a child makes little or no progress, even when additional support has been given or when they consistently work or behave at a level well below that which is expected of a child of a similar age.

When concerns are raised about a child, it is important to gather together as much information as possible, from parents,

records of assessment and, importantly, from first-hand observations of the child in a range of situations. A written format for recording initial concern is useful, in particular to help you and the child's key worker decide upon further action.

## What next?

It is important to remember that the identification of a special educational need aids appropriate provision and this is the key to early intervention. From your observation and assessment, it will become clear what each child needs and how they differ from others in the group and this information will help the key worker when planning and providing suitable activities.

The Code of Practice suggests that where practitioners consider a child has a special educational need, they should plan Early Years Action to meet those needs, aiming at overcoming the child's difficulties as far as possible. Many children will have their needs met in this way as staff are able to use their experience of meeting the individual needs of all the children in their care.

Encourage staff to use the *Curriculum Guidance for the Foundation Stage* when planning appropriate provision. The stepping stones help in clearly identifying components of tasks and these can be further broken down to produce smaller steps for children with special needs.

Throughout, it is important to talk to parents and involve them in your planning. This shared knowledge will lead to action and the earlier the action, the more effective it is likely to be in helping the child progress.

Sue Fisher, early years training consultant.

# Possible indicators of special educational needs

This list provides a starting point. It is important to stress to staff, however, that whilst a check-list can be a useful aid, their own experience and what they observe and understand from this is far more important than a label

## Cognition and learning difficulties
- Concern over fine/gross motor skills
- Language difficulties
- Difficulty following instructions
- Open to distractions
- Works slowly/poor output
- Makes more progress when individual attention is given or when tasks are broken down into small steps

## Behavioural, emotional and social difficulties
- Tearfulness, anti-social, uncooperative
- Withdrawn, isolation from peers, preoccupied
- Aggressive, angry, disruptive
- Hyperactive
- Low self-esteem

## Communication and interaction difficulties (including autistic spectrum disorders)
- Problems with communicating through speech
- Limited speech and vocabulary
- Frustration and anxieties
- Stammering, speech difficult to understand
- Difficulty in understanding meaning of spoken word
- Difficulty in following instructions

## Sensory and physical difficulties
- Poor hand/eye coordination
- Inappropriate answers given to questions
- Immature speech sounds
- Poor sound discrimination
- Difficulty in some aspects of movement

# Providing for all children: differentiation, consolidation and extension

**Within any early years setting, there will be wide variations amongst the children in terms of development and maturity as well as family, religious and cultural background and special needs. All children joining your group or class will therefore have differing experiences, interests, skills and knowledge which will affect the way in which - and the pace at which - they learn.**

You need to be aware of the importance of planning to meet a diversity of needs and to support staff in providing appropriately for all children in your care including those whose difficulties may be able to be addressed through a differentiated curriculum. The revised Code of Practice states that a graduated approach should be developed to help children who have special educational needs. Differentiating the curriculum, thus providing for each child's needs, will be the first step in this model of action and intervention.

All children within a group can be supported in their learning alongside each other as long as staff are aware of these differences as well as each child's stage of development and plan carefully, building on and extending children's knowledge, experiences, interests and skills.

*Guidance for the Foundation Stage* is a valuable document in supporting planning for varying developmental stages of children.

## Planning for all children

To endeavour to meet the needs of all children and aim for each child to reach their full potential, it is essential that teaching is planned and organised effectively to develop all children's knowledge, understanding and skills, while working towards the Early Learning Goals in all six areas of learning.

Plans need to be flexible to allow children to be involved in different ways and at different levels, and whilst you should be aware of the learning intentions from activities, thorough consideration should be given to individual pace and style. These needs can then be used as a starting point for planning, reflecting the differing interests and developmental stages of children and setting challenging yet realistic expectations. The *Curriculum*

## Putting plans into practice

When putting planned activities and experiences into practice, staff should maintain high expectations for each child, making sure that their existing knowledge and understanding is recognised, used and extended, and that challenges are meaningful as well as achievable, encouraging the children to think.

Staff who have a thorough grasp of child development, and the needs of individual children in their care, will be able to use the stepping stones towards the ELGs and pitch expectation correctly for the majority of children, matching teaching to each child's stage of learning and supporting their progression. For some children stepping stones may need breaking down into smaller steps or additional steps created leading up to the stepping stones.

Children sometimes also need to set their own challenges and practise and develop their own skills. In this way, they will gain an understanding of their own abilities and strengths.

## Working with mixed age groups

Many settings work with a wide age range of children within the same group. For these the *Curriculum Guidance* will be of particular benefit in planning activities. In such settings it is particularly easy to fail older, more able children in an attempt to make activities accessible to all. By taking individual levels as a starting point for planning, staff can be confident that all children will learn from activities planned.

## Using the stepping stones to support all children

The *Curriculum Guidance* suggests stepping stones towards a variety of Early Learning Goals in the six areas of learning and these

## Stepping stones

Investigate construction materials.
Realise tools can be used for a purpose.



Join construction pieces together to build and balance.
Begin to try out a range of tools and techniques safely.



Construct with a purpose in mind, using a variety of resources.
Use simple tools and techniques competently and appropriately.



Build and construct with a wide range of objects, selecting appropriate resources, and adapting their work where necessary.
Select the tools and techniques they need to shape, assemble and join materials they are using.

## Activities/extension

Handle a range of card tubes/boxes. Explore different materials. With support appropriate to need, apply glue with brush or glue stick to stick pieces together. Provide a range of opportunities to practise these skills.

Select from a range of resources and experiment with methods of fixing together, beginning to explore joining techniques. Provide opportunities to practise cutting skills - using playdough or fine card to develop skills.
At this stage, staff should observe carefully to make sure the right equipment is introduced at appropriate times, whilst ensuring children are not overwhelmed too early.

Select own resources and use different materials, ie for decoration as well as a variety of tools and methods of joining and building.
Staff should discuss ideas with children, encouraging them to plan and begin to construct with a purpose in mind - some children will begin to 'design' on paper.

Design something more complex, experimenting with temporary and permanent ways of joining paper and card. Provide the children with more freedom to select, review and adapt ideas, supporting them to experiment and develop coordination.
Provide a range of supporting extension activities.

---

stepping stones identify developing knowledge, skills, understanding and attitudes that children need if they are to achieve the ELGs by the end of the Foundation Stage. For some children, these stepping stones will need breaking down into smaller steps, whilst others may appear to miss stages altogether.

I have examined one particular goal (see above) in an attempt to identify ways in which we can provide for the diversity of children in our care. The selected goal belongs to the area of learning covering Knowledge and Understanding of the World and states:

'Build and construct with a wide range of objects, selecting appropriate resources and adapting their work where necessary. Select the tools and techniques they need to shape, assemble and join materials they are using.'

This provides all children with the opportunity to explore and experiment, interpret and represent thoughts and knowledge and express themselves imaginatively and creatively. Using the stepping stones towards this goal, we can explore how a design and technology activity can be differentiated to support all these stages. The activity involves modelling with junk materials.

This activity should be planned to allow children to approach it in different ways according to their needs and interests. The adult role will differ throughout and may lessen in the later stages but intervention may be necessary to avoid children becoming frustrated and abandoning the activity, as well as to encourage them to think and extend their learning.

In providing a high quality curriculum that provides for the needs of all children, we

must first understand how children learn, their individual needs, knowledge and interests and build on this knowledge to ensure each child receives the type and level of stimulus for which they are developmentally ready. We need to offer curriculum experiences which will challenge without overwhelming, remembering that children are capable of much as long as situations provided are meaningful and support children in beginning to make a range of choices and decisions.

It is our role to ensure that we support each individual child to work at an appropriate level as they develop understanding and solutions to the problems they encounter.

Sue Fisher, early years training consultant.

# Early Years Action and **Action Plus**

The revised Code of Practice states that settings should adopt a graduated approach to providing specific help for individual children.

Your setting will already be providing a differentiated curriculum to meet the needs of most of the children you work with each day. If you feel it is necessary to provide additional or different types of support to a particular child, you should consider meeting their needs through Early Years Action.

As SENCO, it is important to remind staff that children progress at different rates and to consider what is reasonable to expect an individual child to achieve. Through working with that child, observing and assessing their progress, staff will be alerted to individual difficulties. In these cases, additional or different action will need to be taken to help the child to progress.

The Code of Practice defines adequate progress as progress that, for example, closes the attainment gap between the child and his peers and ensures access to the full curriculum. The Code also identifies triggers for intervention through Early Years Action when children are making little or no progress. It may be that the child's parents also feel that their child is making little progress and staff working with the child should consult parents at this stage before seeking further support.

At this point, staff should consult you as SENCO and together you should try to gather all the information you are able to about the child through observation, assessment and discussions with the child's parents.

## Early Years Action
You will now need to make sure that the setting and the child's parents co-operate and agree on the action needed to support the child in making progress.

The Code of Practice states that for a child whose needs are to be met through Early Years Action, support could include:

■ Extra adult time in devising the nature

of the planned intervention and monitoring its effectiveness;

■ Providing different learning materials or specific equipment;

■ Some individual or group support;

■ Staff development and training to introduce more effective strategies.

It may be that you are able to provide this training or you may need to seek more specialist advice from relevant organisations or support services.

When a decision has been made on what action will be needed to support the child's progress, it is likely you will consider drawing up an Individual Education Plan (IEP). This is particularly important in recording the strategies you are going to use.

The IEP should contain information on targets set for the child, the teaching strategies and provision to be put in place and a date for review of progress. Details of this progress can then be added at the review.

## Early Years Action Plus
It is important to carry out regular reviews of the child's progress with parents and colleagues. If after these reviews you feel the child is still not making progress, you will probably need to seek additional advice from outside agencies. It is also possible that some children may already be at this stage when they join your setting. Even when outside agencies are involved you, as SENCO, will continue to take the leading role, alongside the child's teacher/key worker.

The Code of Practice states that the practitioner who works day to day with the child, and the SENCO, should be given advice and support from outside specialists. Early Years Action Plus is characterised by this involvement and external support services will be able to provide support and advice on target setting, strategies, materials and resources. It is important to research the type of support available within your

own LEA/EYDCP and familiarise yourself with relevant contacts.

## Referrals to outside agencies
It is your responsibility to make initial contact and forward copies of the records you have collated (with parents' consent). These should include IEPs, reviews, observations and assessments. This will help in establishing what support has already been provided and how.

Using this information and their own observations of the child, they will then be able to offer advice on suitable strategies to use to support the child in working towards these targets. This can then be used when drawing up the child's next IEP. From now on you will have the support of outside agencies in monitoring and reviewing the child's progress.

## Individual Education Plans
All children placed on Early Years Action, Early Years Action Plus and those with a statement of special educational needs should have an Individual Education Plan or IEP. An IEP is a working document which enables you to plan individually for children with special educational needs, detailing what is additional to or different from what you usually provide. IEPs should be easy to understand and form an effective working document for everyone who works with the child.

As SENCO, it is your responsibility to oversee the development of IEPs, although you may not be expected to write each one. This will depend on the requirements of your setting but you will certainly be expected to support the child's key worker in setting appropriate targets and strategies. All IEPs should be shared by everyone working with the child.

## What should an IEP contain?
The major role of the IEP is to set targets for the child. These targets will be decided upon based on a thorough assessment of the child's needs and progress to date. It is important to involve the child, parents, staff and any other professionals working with

the child in setting targets that are realistic and achievable.

## How should targets be set?

When setting targets, it is worth considering the SMART technique to make sure targets are:

Specific
Measurable
Achievable
Relevant
Timebound

Targets will vary according to the child's individual needs. For most children, targets will reflect the need to break down tasks into manageable steps. During the Foundation Stage, it is likely that targets for some children will include aspects of dressing, eating and other areas of personal independence. Remember, however, to make sure that targets are ones you hope the child will achieve within the timescale of the IEP. The teaching strategies to be used and additional provision or resources needed to support the child in achieving set targets will also need to be noted.

## Reviewing IEPs

It is important to continually review progress towards targets, with more formal reviews being held termly. The Code of Practice states that IEPs should be reviewed regularly and at least three times a year.

All relevant parties need to be involved in the review process. Parents' views on their child's progress must be sought and they should be consulted when reviewing targets and setting new ones. It may be difficult to involve the child but parents will be able to reflect their needs and feelings. If outside professionals are involved, they may not be able to attend every meeting but you can still involve them in the review process by asking for updated information in a written format or through a telephone discussion.

When all this information has been gathered you will be able to consider the progress the child has made and the effectiveness of the IEP and take into account any new information or advice when setting targets for the next IEP.

There is no set format for IEPs. Your local education authority may have their own system and a sample one is provided for you in this book on page 62. You are likely to find that the most effective IEP is one you devise yourself as this will be suited to your setting and the children attending.

Sue Fisher, early years training consultant.

---

**Sample IEP**

# Individual Education Plan

**For:** Sam Fisher          **D.O.B:** 10.02.98

(Early Years Action) / Action Plus / Statement of SEN

**Period of plan:** Summer term      **Date:** 20.04.02

| Strengths / interests | Learning needs |
|---|---|
| Hand – eye co-ordination – loves jigsaws, Lego, sand. Enjoys investigative play. Good computer skills. | Usually plays alone. Short concentration span in group work/story time. |

| Targets | Strategies |
|---|---|
| To play alongside other children. To join a group story session. | Remove obvious distractions. Offer support and praise. Encourage Sam to play in role-play area / areas of co-operative play. |

| Resources | Monitoring, assessment and success criteria |
|---|---|
| Role play/dressing up. Sand and water play. Outdoor play house. Additional staff support at story time. | Record weekly observations and monthly updates towards targets. Record in profile. |

**Agreed by:** _____ SENCO

_____ Parent

**Date for review:** 20.07.02

# *Statutory* **assessment** and **statements**

There will be a small number of children for whom the support you give through Early Years Action Plus will not be effective enough to enable the child to make satisfactory progress. If it is considered that the child has long-term needs, the local education authority may consider carrying out a statutory assessment leading to a statement of special educational needs. However, this will only be the case for no more than two per cent of children.

As SENCO, if you, in consultation with the child's teacher/key worker, their parents and other professionals involved, feel they would benefit from a statutory assessment you will be able to request this. Likewise parents or other professionals involved with the child are also able to make a referral. Statutory assessments are multi-disciplinary, in other words, they involve everyone working with the child. So regardless of who makes the initial request, you will be contacted for your opinions.

## Asking for an assessment

Your local education authority should have a named person to contact if you are considering asking for a statutory assessment. The LEA will be able to tell you who to contact and how. Who carries out this role will depend on how your LEA is organised. They will be able to give you advice on the process, supply the relevant forms and explain how to fill them in.

The type of information you will be asked for will include details of the child's difficulties and needs, what action has been taken to date and strategies employed, probably through Early Years Action and Early Years Action Plus, and details of any outside advice obtained and support received. It is important that you provide all this information so that the LEA can seek advice from the appropriate people.

In determining whether a statutory assessment is necessary, the LEA will consider all the information supplied, and in particular:

■ The difficulties you have identified;

■ The strategies you have put in place through Early Years Action and Early Years Action Plus;

■ Parents' views;

■ Opinions and information from outside agencies.

The LEA must make an assessment of all this information within six weeks and decide whether they feel they have enough evidence to carry out a statutory assessment. They will only do so if they feel that the child's needs are only likely to be fully addressed through a statement of special educational needs. The key to this decision is usually based on whether these needs are seen as long-term needs that are likely to continue to require attention throughout all or most of their school life.

If the LEA decides to proceed with the statement they will contact you again for more information. A draft statement will then be issued, followed by the final statement. The whole process must be completed within six months.

## What happens if a request is refused?

If a request is refused, the LEA must contact the person who made the request and explain, in writing, why the decision was made. If you continue to feel that the child is not making satisfactory progress, you can contact the LEA again after the next review of the child's IEP. If, after receiving further reports, the LEA agrees that the child does require extra support, they will write a statement for that child. Briefly, this will contain:

■ Details of the child's needs

■ The additional help they need

■ How this will be monitored

For most children, it will be possible to provide this additional help in the setting with support from your LEA. Your setting will then be named in the statement and

*'A statement ... should provide additional support for the child at this stage as well as helping them prepare for school and making sure the child's needs are provided for during their school years.'*

the LEA will fund the additional provision specified in the statement.

You will need to make sure that you inform staff of the content of the statement and how it is to be implemented.

## How might a statement support a child?

The type of additional support likely to be detailed in a statement includes the involvement of a support worker to provide:

■ additional one-to-one support;

■ individualised support;

■ support with planning;

■ support in developing IEPs and reviewing progress.

In some cases, the statement may specify additional equipment to support the child and help them to access the full curriculum and activities.

It is a misconception that additional support hours are always provided as the LEA will decide upon the most appropriate support to meet the child's needs.

## Statement reviews

When children move out of the Foundation Stage, their statements will be reviewed annually. The early years, however, is a time of rapid growth, development and change, so reviews should be carried out six monthly to ensure the provision being made is still appropriate to the child's needs. A statement can be amended after a six monthly review to reflect significant changes if necessary.

As SENCO, it is likely that you will take the lead in organising the review, which can be timed to coincide with the termly review of the child's IEP. The timescale above (see box) can be used as a guide to organising and carrying out reviews.

A statement can be a valuable aid to progress for a child with special educational needs during the early years. It should provide additional support for the child at this stage as well as helping them prepare for school and making sure the child's needs are provided for during their school years.

Sue Fisher, early years training consultant.

## Suggested timescale

### Before the review

**Six weeks -** invite parents, support staff, key workers and outside professionals involved with the child to attend.

**Two weeks -** request any written reports from professionals involved with the child to be submitted by this date.

**Two weeks -** send copies of these reports to all invited parties.

### The review meeting
It is likely that you, the SENCO, will chair the meeting.

### After the review
The information gathered should be collated on to a special review form (provided by the LEA) and sent to the LEA and all parties involved in the review.

The review form will ask whether there are any significant changes in the child's development and needs, whether the statement is still required and the main targets for the child. After reviewing the statement, it is still important to set out these targets in a new IEP. The review form should then be sent to the LEA who will circulate it with reports and copies of the new IEP attached.

# Record keeping, planning *and* assessment

Record keeping is an important part of working with young children and all the more so when working with children with special educational needs.

The revised Code of Practice states that monitoring individual children's progress throughout the Foundation Stage is essential. It is the responsibility of each setting to decide the exact procedures to adopt and paperwork to use. The crucial factor is that it should support everyone in offering the best quality provision to each child.

Whilst Individual Education Plans are important for children already identified as having special educational needs, the system you adopt for assessment of attainment and progress is valuable in recording information on all children's progress and may help in providing evidence that a child is experiencing difficulties in learning. It should also provide a guide to how suitable your provision is for children with special educational needs through the progress they make.

Using a familiar system is likely to help staff feel more confident. However, as SENCO, you may feel that a new system should be put into place. If so, make sure this is positive, reflecting achievement rather that highlighting what the child cannot do.

This can be achieved for most children by breaking learning objectives down into small steps and recording the achievement of each step rather than just the overall objective. Questionnaires to parents should support assessments and help to provide a starting point for working with the child. Remember, too, that these records should include regular information on progress from parents and from other organisations involved to produce an overall picture of the child and their achievements.

## Involving children

It is good practice to involve all children in the assessment of their progress. Children enjoy talking about what they have achieved and looking at examples of their work and photographic evidence, particularly if they

appear in them! All these things encourage a sense of pride in their achievements.

How you involve children is a matter for you and your colleagues to decide but systems are most valuable and enjoyable when they are child centred and play based.

## The importance of observation

Staff should be encouraged to carry out regular observations of the children in a range of situations and activities. For children with IEPs, these may be linked to particular targets. Through these observations, staff will be able to keep written notes of progress towards these targets. These can be brief bullet point notes but, kept regularly, they will provide valuable information which can be brought forward at the next review of the child's progress. If a target is not met, these notes may also help to highlight why.

## Additional records to consider

Occasionally, staff members may raise a

concern about a child's development or behaviour. In this case it is worth considering using an 'expression of concern' format to record written observations on the child (see page 61). This will provide useful evidence if you feel the child needs to have their needs met through Early Years Action or to support staff in providing more successfully for the child through a differentiated curriculum.

You will need to share record keeping responsibilities with staff. An additional record you may wish to keep could take the form of a diary sheet in date order to record brief details of all formal and informal meetings with parents and other professionals supporting the child, telephone calls and any other relevant information. This will provide an 'at a glance' check on decisions made.

## Planning and organisation

Encourage staff to use their observations of children to involve them in planning. Through observing children at play, staff will be able to assess what children enjoy most and are most interested in as well as what fails to stimulate their interest. This knowledge and that gained from discussion with parents and other relevant people will help staff to plan around children's interests. Encourage staff to have high expectations and yet to pitch activities at just the right level for success. This will help build confidence and self-esteem.

## Providing an inclusive environment

Early years practitioners will recognise the importance of making everyone feel included, settled and secure.

As SENCO, you can support staff in providing an inclusive environment through:

- providing teaching materials and books which cater for a wide range of abilities;

- talking to children about special educational needs - what it means and the forms it can take;

- helping children to think about and care for others;

- providing opportunities for each child to feel included and valued, such as through circle time activities.

- supporting children to develop positive attitudes through being a good role model;

- involving parents in children's learning and developing strong links with home;

- using teaching strategies which ensure all children are able to participate in activities (with modification, if necessary and individual approaches);

- showing realistic, consistent expectations for children's behaviour;

- using additional support if available to encourage children to join in and benefit from being part of a group.

## Staff training

An important part of the SENCO's role is to provide training for other staff members. At first, it is likely that you will cover such areas as SEN awareness and inclusion, identification and assessment of special educational needs, the Code of Practice recommendations and requirements and special needs policy.

Additional training needs will become apparent from time to time, particularly when a member of staff is working with a child who has a specific condition or difficulty. You will need to support this member of staff by providing relevant information and helping to organise specialist training.

Your Early Years Development and Childcare Partnership may produce a local handbook or directory. Alternatively, you could contact local colleges, health authorities or training providers for details of relevant training. It is worth collating all information on training opportunities sent to you even if you do not feel it is relevant at the time. You will then know who to contact if the need does arise in the future.

The contacts you have made with other professionals through working with children with special educational needs will also prove a valuable resource in providing information or offering training.

# Working with parents of children with special needs

As SENCO, it is your responsibility to ensure that your intentions regarding working in partnership with parents are outlined in your setting's special educational needs policy and that this is reflected in practice throughout the setting.

The Code of Practice recognises the importance of the role of parents in their child's education. Parents know their child best. They have a wealth of knowledge and experience to share about their child's development and needs. Early years practitioners must encourage parents to share their knowledge and any concerns they may have, both about their child's needs and the provision being made for them.

## Partnership in practice

For such a partnership to be achieved effectively, it is important that both parties recognise and value each others contributions. The Code of Practice recognises that parents have responsibilities for communicating with staff working with their child. Remind staff that they must always respect parents' views and opinions and be sensitive towards their feelings. Some staff members will probably need to work on their own communication skills and extend their understanding of working with parents, sometimes in difficult situations. As SENCO, you will need to monitor this and seek or provide suitable training if such a need should arise.

It is vitally important to remember the pressure that parents may be under due to their child's special needs. They may be experiencing feelings of guilt and rejection, resulting in a loss of confidence or self-esteem. Some, particularly where the child has an emotional or behavioural difficulty, may feel they have been held responsible for this and may appear angry or over-sensitive.

Encourage staff to develop empathy with these parents, helping them to feel at ease, and hopefully find it easier to share concerns about their child. Remind them that some parents may have great difficulty in coming to terms with their child's special needs, and that approaches for dealing with

these needs will differ. Some parents may place heavy emphasis on a child's disability, whilst others may play down their child's difficulties and emphasise the positive.

Whatever their own feelings, staff must respect all views and work positively and equally well with all parents. Even very young children are aware of how staff feel and respond to their parents. It is of utmost importance that staff value the input of parents and ensure they feel that their child is accepted and valued, too.

## Building a picture of each child's needs

It is important to listen to parents' views at first to help you build up a picture of their child based on previous experiences. It is also important to establish what the child may think. This is usually difficult to find out directly with very young children, but it can be done indirectly through discussion with those who are closest to them.

Before a child with special educational needs starts at your setting, arrange a home visit if possible to observe the child in their own environment. This also gives you an opportunity to discuss any issues with parents in a relaxed, familiar environment. Parents should also be given the chance to visit the setting on their own as well as with their child before the child starts to attend. This will help you when drawing up an individualised learning programme to take into account care and educational needs and provide targets and opportunities for them to develop in the six areas of learning.

After this, meeting with parents regularly, including informally, will help to ensure they are able to update you on their child's care needs and provide the latest information on others involved in their

*'A strong partnership will develop if parents feel that their knowledge of their child and their opinions are listened to and valued and that they and their child are made to feel welcome by you and your staff team.'*

care such as Portage workers and speech therapists. Importantly, too, it will provide opportunities to share observations on their child's progress.

The timing of meetings and IEP reviews can be difficult for some parents. Many children attending private day nurseries have working parents and others may need to make childcare arrangements for other children whilst they attend a meeting. It is, therefore, important to take into account the individual needs of parents and be flexible about appointments.

### Sharing achievement

Remember that it is just as important to share the child's achievements as it is to voice your concerns. It can raise the confidence and self-esteem of both child and parents and could be as simple as drawing attention to the child's painting displayed on the wall, to a book or toy the child has shown particular interest in or celebrating a new stage of development the child has reached - for example, playing alongside other children or beginning to share resources.

Achievement for many children with special educational needs will need to be measured in much smaller steps than usual but this does not make their progress any less successful. Emphasise the child's strengths, sharing positive comments with both parents and child.

You will need to develop different methods of sharing achievement for parents who are not able to come in to your setting regularly. Many early years settings are familiar with home/nursery diaries and use these as an effective way of sharing information on the child's successes and experiences. This can be a valuable two-way link when it is not possible to have regular face-to-face contact with parents.

### Parent partnership services and additional support

Make sure that parents are fully aware of the local parent partnership service and how they can get advice and support from this service. This service is offered by each LEA and aims to give practical, impartial advice to parents and carers of children with special educational needs as well as support and information which will help parents play an active role in making decisions concerning their child's education. The parent partnership service should offer a range of services, including access to an individual parent supporter for all parents who want one and putting families in touch with local support groups.

Individual parental supporters are trained volunteers who can also support parents in completing paperwork and accompanying them to meetings or on visits to schools.

Some local education authorities/early years development and childcare partnerships have produced their own comprehensive directories of local support groups and relevant organisations. As a SENCO, however, it is good practice to build your own directory of local and national contacts to support staff as well as parents.

### Moving on

Throughout all stages of a child's early care and education, parental involvement is essential and it is important that this continues when the child moves on to primary school. Records kept on a child with special educational needs, including individual education plans/learning programmes should be passed on to the school, with the parents' consent. You may need to explain the benefits to the child of passing these records on.

A strong partnership will develop if parents feel that their knowledge of their child and their opinions are listened to and valued and that they and their child are made to feel welcome by you and your staff team.

Sue Fisher, early years training consultant.

## Useful publications and contacts

*Special Educational Needs - A Guide for Parents* (DfES Ref 0800/2001) A free leaflet available from DfES Publications. Tel: 0845 6022260 or email dfes@prolog.uk.com

Contact a Family (CAF), 209-211 City Road, London EC1V 1JN Tel: 020 7608 8700 Provides support and advice to parents of children with special needs. Also operates a Freephone Helpline: 0808 808 3555 Mon-Fri 10am-4pm

Advisory Centre for Education (ACE), Unit 1B, Aberdeen Studios, 22 Highbury Grove, London N5 2DQ. Tel: 0207 354 8321 Also Freephone Helpline 0808 800 5793 2-5pm weekdays A national advice centre for parents offering information and support about state education in England and Wales for five-to sixteen-year-olds. Offers advice on many topics including special educational needs. Advice is also available on their website at: www.ace-ed.org.uk

DIAL UK (Disablement Information and Advice Lines), St Catherines, Tickhill Road, Doncaster DN4 8QN. Supports a network of local disablement information and advice officers. Telephone 01302 310123 to find out who your local officer is.

Home-Start UK, 2 Salisbury Road, Leicester LE1 7QR. Tel: 0116 233 9955. www.home-start.org.uk

National Portage Association, PO Box 3075, Yeovil, Somerset BA21 3FB. Tel: 01935 471641

# Working with
# **other professionals**

Through developing relationships with a range of professionals and organisations, you will be able to build links between families of children with special educational needs in your setting and those people who are able to offer them support. For many parents, this will be a difficult time and by helping in this way you will not only be ensuring the best support possible for the child, but also for the whole family.

## What role might other professionals play?

Where you have decided that children's needs can be met through Early Years Action, or when initial concern is raised about a child's progress, it is likely that your contact with outside agencies will be mainly an information gathering exercise.

For children whose needs will be met through Early Years Action Plus and for those with a statement of special educational needs, other professionals/organisations will be named on relevant documentation and should work in partnership with you to offer support for the child and join in setting targets for achievement.

For some children, particularly those with a statement of special educational needs, other professionals, such as Portage workers, may visit your setting to advise staff and work with individual children. A statement may also identify the need for a support worker who will be employed or sub-contracted by the local education authority. Whilst their main role will be to support the child with special educational needs, everyone involved can reap rewards from this partnership. The most beneficial approach is for staff to work as a team in providing for all children, involving the support worker where possible, for example, in the planning of activities.

## Establishing and maintaining contact

It is worth doing some homework to find out not only which organisations will be able to provide some support but also who the key people in each department are and how they can be contacted. Getting in

touch with them could be your first step towards building a successful working relationship. We all like to hear a familiar voice at the end of the phone so remember to keep a record of such contacts and keep this information updated as contacts change.

It is also useful to collect information on local resources, such as toy libraries. How these are organised will differ from area to area and your local toy library may be run by social services, health services or a voluntary organisation such as the Pre-school Learning Alliance. Specialist toy libraries are available in some areas, but all toy libraries provide a wide range of toys and equipment aimed at developing individual skills as well as some specific resources suitable for children with differing special needs.

Your Early Years Development and Childcare Partnership, local education authority, health service or other local body may already have a directory of useful local contacts. Remember also to collect information on relevant national support groups and organisations. There are many such groups, so a good starting point would be to contact those particularly relevant to the children and families you are currently working with or expect to work with in the near future.

If possible, display a selection of information leaflets from these groups. This will help to make sure that parents are not singled out and will provide helpful information when a parent suspects their child may have a special need or when this has been suggested to them.

## Issues to consider

It will be beneficial to all parties if you:

■ Make sure you have a designated contact with lead responsibility for liaison with other professionals - this is likely to be the child's key worker (alongside the SENCO) as they will have particular knowledge of the child's needs and be known to the parents.

■ Set up a regular means of two-way communication - consider informal contact by telephone/email as well as more formal meetings.

■ Invite them to review meetings - encourage involvement in both the meeting and participation in setting targets.

■ Make sure copies of IEPs are given/sent to all professionals involved.

■ Think about the timing of meetings - as with parents, remember those invited will have other commitments. It is good practice to find out what times are particularly good/difficult before arranging meetings. You will need to develop a flexible approach to involve all relevant parties.

The chart provided (see right) gives brief information on some of the professionals you are most likely to come into contact with. This list is not exhaustive and you will be able to extend this over time by adding your own. It should, however, provide a useful resource for recording and updating relevant contacts.

Sue Fisher, early years training consultant.

| Contact name | Help available | Contact details |
| --- | --- | --- |
| Educational psychologist | Helps to determine what child's educational difficulties may be and suggest relevant teaching approaches. Can also give advice on behaviour management (will always be involved if a child is to be statutorily assessed prior to a statement of SEN). | _____ _____ _____ |
| Social worker | Can offer home support/assessment if needed. | _____ |
| Speech and language therapist | Will assess child and offer advice to both parent and setting. May develop specific programmes for the child/suggest targets for inclusion on IEPs. May provide regular or one-off support dependent on need. | _____ _____ |
| Individual support worker | Provides help in developing and maintaining individualised programme of support for child (not necessarily 1:1 teaching). This support is often provided for children with a statement of SEN. Some EYDCPs/LEAs may also provide this for those without a statement – particularly for those with emotional/behavioural difficulties. | _____ _____ _____ |
| Portage worker | Provides a home teaching scheme for pre-school children with SEN. Worker will assess child's level of development and decide which skills to work on next. May visit setting to observe how child behaves in a different environment. | _____ _____ |
| Physiotherapist | Provides support for children with physical difficulties/delay or poor motor control. Provides an individually planned programme of movements or exercises to be carried out at home/setting. Offers support and advice on specialist equipment. | _____ _____ |
| Clinical psychologist | Provides support, counselling and therapy for families. Can also offer advice on behaviour management, cognitive development and development assessment. | _____ _____ |

# What is **Portage?**

Portage is a scheme for teaching pre-school children with special needs new and useful skills in their own home, through making their parents more effective teachers of their children. It originated in the USA in the 1960s, in Portage, Wisconsin, and was introduced into the UK in 1976.

There are now around 150 registered Portage services throughout the country that meet the criteria as laid down by the National Portage Association. Services work with children with a range of special needs, including Down's Syndrome, cerebral palsy, and autism, as well as children with visual or hearing problems and language delay or disorder.

## National Portage Association

For more information about the National Portage Association, visit the Portage website at www.portage.org.uk or contact
The Administrator
NPA
PO Box 3075
Yeovil BA21 3FB
Tel: 01935 471641

Portage services vary considerably from region to region. They may be funded through education, health or social services, or be joint funded. A Portage team may include people from a variety of backgrounds, such as teaching, speech and language therapy, community nursing and health visiting.

Some services have volunteer home visitors; these are often past Portage parents. To become a Portage home visitor, you have to undertake a Portage Basic Workshop which lasts the equivalent of three days. It looks at the core principles of the Portage approach, as well as how to use the Portage materials to make assessments, to select teaching targets and long-term goals and to keep records.

### How does Portage work?

Parents have a major role in choosing and carrying out the weekly tasks that encourage their child to develop skills in a variety of areas. During the first few weekly visits the home visitor and the parent will use the Portage check-list to identify what skills the child already has, those that are emerging and what the priorities are for the next few months. The check-list covers development up to the age of six in social, self-help, cognitive, motor and language skills, and a picture of the child's strengths and weaknesses is built up.

Together the parent and the home visitor decide on appropriate long-term goals, and activities to promote these goals are rehearsed each week for the parent to practise throughout the following week. These activities are written down on activity charts that carefully identify all the aspects that need to be considered, such as:

■ a clear description of what the adult and child will do;

■ what toys will be used;

■ what help it might be necessary to give the child; and

■ what rewards will be given.

*'It is also important to recognise and build on the things that the child can do and enjoys, as so often the messages about the child have been negative and based on what he or she can't do.'*

The activity charts are used to record the progress during the week and over a period of time.

This might sound rather formal and clinical, but in practice it isn't. Parents want to know what they can do for their child, but often feel they do not know where to start. It is often necessary to break down an individual skill into smaller parts that are more achievable, and this can be difficult to do at first. However, it is important so that even small steps towards the goal are recognised and celebrated. It is also important to recognise and build on the things that the child can do and enjoys, as so often the messages about the child have been negative and based on what he or she can't do.

The regular weekly visits mean that there is constant feedback between the parent and home visitor. The relationship that is developed through this contact means that some weeks the home visitor spends more time listening to the parents' feelings than talking about the activities, but this is a very important aspect of Portage support.

The parent and home visitor choose activities that are based on play, and which can be incorporated easily into the daily routines of the household. Other members of the family become involved, including brothers and sisters who often play an important part in the activities. Parents become more competent and confident about their teaching, more articulate about their child's skills and more aware of the different ways that children learn. As one

parent says, 'The Portage method gave us the specific tools to help (our son) progress. No longer did I feel that we were working towards unobtainable goals, for I was helped merely to work towards the next, the closest milestone, and have confidence that having reached it, the following one would be attained as well. Looking back it seems as if there was a miracle, although I know there was a lot of hard work as well. Somehow the Portage activities never seemed a burden – we just included them into our daily routines and found that they served to enrich our family life.' (from *To A Different Drumbeat: A practical Guide to Parenting Children with Special Needs* by Clarke, Kofsky, Lauruol Hawthorn Press 1989 ISBN 1 869890 09 4)

The positive reports of registered Portage services that have been inspected under the nursery education scheme have identified the strong partnership with parents and the effective assessment and recording processes as particular strengths.

## What contact might Portage have with other settings?
When the time comes for a child to become involved in a group outside his home, for example his local playgroup or day nursery, you may well have contact with his Portage visitor. Effective liaison is one of the fundamental aspects of the Portage approach.

The home visitor could be involved in a number of ways. She might visit the group with the child in the initial stages or call in to see how things are going as time passes. She may discuss his current long-term goals with you, and how to approach some of them in your setting. This may be helpful to you when drawing up an individual education plan. She will ask for your observations of the child's progress in particular areas so that a full picture can be gathered, especially when it is time to review the long-term goals.

Over the years the Portage model has been adopted in countries around the world and adapted into many different settings, other than the home. In response to the many pre-school children with special needs who are attending non-specialist provision, and in recognition of the implications of the Code of Practice for the Identification and Assessment of Special Educational Needs, the National Portage Association has produced a training package called *Quality Play*. The aim of the course is to raise awareness that all children, including those with a special need or disability, have rights to effective participation in a wide range of play experiences. It looks at ways to help practitioners working in group situations, such as playgroups and day nurseries, to develop strategies aimed at analysing and supporting the play of individual children of all abilities. The approach links closely to the stages in the Code of Practice.

There are continuous developments in the Portage delivery. For example, some services are looking at ways of extending aspects of the Portage approach as a child moves on into mainstream school, involving close liaison between the home visitor, parents and school staff. They have developed the Portage goals to include new skills needed for successful transition into school and they also provide training and ongoing support for teachers during the first two terms that the child is in school.

The National Portage Association works to encourage the principles that lie at the heart of Portage. As well as the Basic Workshop, which is open to people who may not be home visitors but who are interested in knowing how the Portage principles can be adapted into their setting, it is continually developing and monitoring further training modules. Examples include autism, play, early motor and communication skills, as well as aspects such as working with children with profound and multiple learning difficulties and the multicultural dimension of Portage.

Glen Cossins has worked for Gloucester Portage and was South West Regional Representative for the National Portage Association.

# Managing
# children's **behaviour**

Children need to learn, often through trial and error, how to behave in an acceptable way in a group setting. However, good behaviour cannot be taught in isolation from the rest of the activities but pervades everything going on in the group. It is important not to see behaviour as a separate issue, but within the wider context of the group, as an integral part of the learning taking place and the overall organisation of the sessions.

Children's behaviour is also influenced by wider social, emotional and cultural factors. How children behave will depend on how the group is organised, the planning of the daily routine, the quality of the activities available, the choices on offer and the quality of the interaction between the adults and children and between the children themselves. Children's behaviour is closely related to relationships. Other factors such as partnership with parents and carers will also have an impact on the children's behaviour in the group.

As the way children behave is such an important factor in their learning, each early years setting should have a written behaviour policy, which is often referred to as a discipline policy. However, managing children's behaviour is not simply about 'discipline', or 'getting them ready for school'. Discipline in the pre-school situation is about having order within the group. It is not about orders to be mindlessly followed, but about helping the children understand right from wrong and helping them learn to behave in appropriate, socially acceptable ways for the rest of their lives.

## What is a policy?
A policy is a working document which clearly explains the group's philosophy, procedures and approaches to managing the children's behaviour on a daily basis. The main reason for having a written policy is to share this information with all those involved in the group to promote consistency. If adults are clear, consistent and fair the children will benefit.

It is important that those involved in

'Now think hard, children. Was leaving Mrs Conway buried overnight in our sand area right or wrong?'

*Reproduced by kind permission of The Daily Mail*

carrying it through in practice have ownership of the policy. In other words, the policy should be something to which staff, parents and even children should have an input, not something written by or imposed from above, or some sort of standard list produced by an organisation or copied from another setting.

A staff meeting is a useful time to brainstorm ideas. A draft could be sent to parents for comments. Each policy will be individual to each group and the content should be developed and discussed by all staff, in response to the group's needs and circumstances. The length of the policy will vary from group to group. The main point is that it should be clear, practical and easy to understand. The whole idea is for unwanted behaviour to happen as little as possible.

## Who is a policy for?
The policy is for the benefit of anyone involved in the running of the group. This includes the staff, parents, volunteers, students, any management committee and, ultimately, the children in the group. A

policy provides clear guidance for the adults in the group on procedures for encouraging wanted behaviour and dealing with unwanted behaviour. Whilst children are often accused of being very good at 'playing adults off' one against the other, they are actually testing out the consistency of boundaries that are being set and can feel confused by inconsistent responses. To give a simple example, if only two children are allowed at the sand tray and one day someone allows three children to play, they become confused, especially if another adult then appears and tells them off! It is important for children to have a minimum number of clear rules which are consistently applied. These could be attached to or included in the policy. Some simple rules can be displayed in pictorial form using matchstick people. Typically, these might include points of routine organisation such as 'four in the sand tray'.

If parents are given a chance to read the policy, they will be clear before their children start attending the group about the procedures which will be followed and any support available in the case of a child with a particular difficulty. The parent may then choose to adopt similar procedures in the home to support the work of the group.

A policy is also a valuable tool for allowing outside agencies, such as Social Services or Ofsted, to see that the group is professionally managed and has given careful thought to this element of learning.

Last, but most important, the children themselves will benefit from the policy. Through its implementation, they will learn the difference between acceptable and unacceptable behaviour and they will learn to take responsibility for the consequences of their actions. They will be helped to develop self-control, respect for the needs of others and respect for property.

## What should the policy contain?

Although there is no such thing as a model policy, there are some points which can be applied to most pre-school groups. As a guide, the policy should contain clear statements on the following points:

- an overview of your group's approach, aims, philosophy
- procedures for encouraging acceptable behaviour
- procedures for dealing with unwanted behaviour
- procedures which are unacceptable for managing behaviour
- any agreed rules
- name of person to contact in case of concerns
- date produced or reviewed

Remember to make sure that new staff are aware of the policy. Staff could be asked to sign to say they have read and agree to implement the policy. It is also important to reflect on how it is working in practice, to review and if necessary update the policy from time to time. Once the policy is in place it needs to be translated into practical situations in the day-to-day organisation of the group.

*Caroline Jones, nursery owner and part-time lecturer at the University of Warwick*

# Sample policy - Happyland Pre-school Group

## Overview
Happyland sets high expectations of behaviour through encouraging and praising good behaviour. At Happylands we encourage children to respect themselves, each other, adults and property. We apply simple rules fairly and consistently. We aim to provide a happy, caring environment with challenging activities. Under no circumstances do we use any form of corporal punishment. In the case of a particular incident or persistent unacceptable behaviour we always discuss ways forward with parents.

Our agreed rules are clearly explained to the children and are on the parents' noticeboard. They are based on the following principle:

- Unwanted behaviour is behaviour likely to hurt, injure or upset another child, himself or an adult. Unwanted behaviour shows a lack of respect for others, disrupts their play and learning or damages their property. Below are our procedures for managing the children's behaviour.

## Positive procedures for encouraging good behaviour
- prevention – anticipation and removal of potential problems (stop the fight before it happens!)
- interaction – plenty of adult attention (so that there's no need to misbehave to attract attention!)
- praise or reward – all adults should offer explicit praise for good behaviour, for example turn taking, co-operation, sharing, listening . . . drawing attention to the good rather than the bad
- provision – provide physically challenging and emotionally satisfying activities for children to 'let off steam'
- clear expectations applied in a positive way – 'No pushing in the line' becomes 'Stand nicely'
- leading by positive examples from adults.

In certain circumstances, such as racist language, physical abuse or dangerous behaviour an instant adult response is required.

## Procedures for dealing with unwanted behaviour
- redirection – distract to another activity or join in with activity
- a firm 'No' and a clear explanation of why the behaviour is unacceptable
- speak calmly, clearly and firmly to gain control
- give a warning of the consequence if the behaviour does not stop
- use the consequence, for example, removal from the situation, or removal of the toy
- a fresh start afterwards

## Unacceptable procedures in managing behaviour
These should never be used and, if seen, would and should be reported immediately to the person in charge. Such conduct could result in staff dismissal.

- shouting, criticism and comparison. Shouting conveys a loss of control.
- labelling the child, rather than the behaviour, as 'naughty' or undesirable
- use of any form of corporal punishment, including smacking, pinching, poking or rough handling
- use of any other humiliating and frightening punishment, including shouting, offensive language, name calling or isolation.

Named person - If you are concerned about any child's behaviour or our responses or have any other comment on this policy please contact:

Date: ........................................

# Establishing **better** behaviour

If a child is misbehaving, the first thing adults need to consider is whether the child is misbehaving deliberately or might there be another reason for his actions. Sometimes adults need to step back and consider the cause of the unwanted behaviour, particularly if a child's behaviour changes from being normally co-operative to difficult. Other reasons for so-called 'naughtiness' may include:

### Expectations or language not matched to stage of development

Interaction with children must take account of their stage of development. Young children can only cope with a limited amount of instructions at any one time and may not be being deliberately disobedient but genuinely not understand what is expected. For example, a child who has limited comprehension or auditory memory will not understand a complex series of instructions such as 'When you've finished, hang up your apron, wash your hands, go to the toilet and then go into the other room' and may end up looking blank when he or she is then told off for not going into the other room. The same child would have responded appropriately to one or two instructions at a time.

*'A child who is tearful or clingy or having a tantrum is not necessarily being naughty.'*

Sometimes they are being asked to do a task which is not matched to their level of understanding. In other words the task is too hard or too easy and they become frustrated, perhaps resulting in a tantrum or a squabble. They may not have heard the instruction the first time and need it repeating. Sometimes, they do not have the language to understand the instruction in the first place. It is easy for an adult to become frustrated or cross when a child appears not to be doing as he or she was told. For example, the instruction 'Find a space' often results in children

wandering around all over the place. Is the adult sure the child knows what a space is? Is the child walking around looking for it? Often a child can be labelled naughty for something which is merely developmental, for example, wetting pants, not sitting still for long, lack of attention, when maybe he or she is just not ready or able to do what is being expected.

### Sheer physical exuberance

If there is not enough outlet for a child's energy he or she may run around, start crawling under the tables, or climb on the furniture. It is important to ensure that if the children cannot go outside, perhaps due to the weather, some alternative form of energetic activity is provided indoors.

*'If a child tells a parent 'Mrs Jones got cross with me today', the parent may phone up wanting to know what's happened. It is professional to take the parent quietly to one side and explain the incident.'*

### Insecurity

Children become confused if adults are inconsistent. They feel insecure if expectations are not made clear or something which is acceptable one day is not accepted the next day. They become confused if the routine changes for any reason or staff changes are taking place. Offering children an open choice may also result in confusion. 'Who wants to go first in the line?' will lead to chaos, whereas with 'It's John's turn to be first today and Joanne's tomorrow' everyone knows what they have to do.

### Illness

Often a change in behaviour can be a sign of developing illness. The child does not feel right but does not know how to express the feelings. He or she becomes miserable and unco-operative, even cheeky. The next day the child develops an ear infection or breaks out in spots!

## Anxiety

Factors outside the group's control may have triggered the unwanted behaviour. Those working with young children are all too familiar with changes in behaviour when something is amiss at home which has upset the child in some way. It may be a way of releasing anxieties – the death of a grandparent, arrival of a new baby, a parent leaving the family home, fear of starting school. Children should be happy and develop relationships with adults and with each other which minimise negative behaviour. If they are encouraged to express anxieties and ask questions the need for anti-social behaviour as a response to anxiety is reduced. Any sudden change in behaviour should always be shared with the parents and monitored carefully by a named adult.

## Anger

A child who is tearful or clingy or having a tantrum is not necessarily being naughty. Tantrums, for example, are very common among toddlers. The child has not yet acquired a sufficient grasp of language to express himself in words. The need to assert independence spills over into a tantrum. A tantrum is a very powerful feeling of anger and frustration and often the child needs comfort combined with restraint. A tantrum is a child's (and some adults'!) way of expressing very strong emotions. Inability to cope with people, things or situations is often the cause. Those working closely with children will recognise a tantrum from a child who is using a loud noise to attract attention and trying to control the adult or getting his or her own way. Responses may vary and will depend on the circumstances. Try to find out what is making the child angry. Often a child's anger can be redirected through playing with dough, role play, hammering pegs, banging a drum, or going out in the garden. Withdrawal to a quiet place or a little cuddle will help him or her regain control. The important thing is for the adult to remain calm and once the tantrum has subsided, to make a fresh start.

## Testing the boundaries

Prevention is better than cure and many things can be avoided if the circumstances which trigger the unwanted behaviour are avoided in the first place. Of course, children will still explore and experiment to find out where the boundaries lie between acceptable and unacceptable behaviour. Where the situation or the adult is unfamiliar they will experiment with different kinds of behaviour until it becomes clear where the line is drawn. Often children look straight at the adult before actually doing the 'crime'! The absence of consistent boundaries leaves children insecure, dashing about waiting for someone to control them. Often they are labelled hyperactive, when really they are seeking boundaries to control their behaviour. Once the children have discovered what is allowed and what isn't allowed and the same rules apply all the time, they will be satisfied and direct their energies elsewhere.

## Positive strategies

Unacceptable behaviour in the pre-school is usually defined as action which interrupts the child's own learning or the learning of others, harms another person, themselves or property. Within a context of positive preventative strategies unwanted behaviour can be dealt with through light control methods, although in some cases stronger measures may be called for. Light control is appropriate in a situation which requires minimum intervention.

One example of light control is where attention is focused on the rest of the group, sometimes known as positively ignoring. This will often succeed in reminding the 'targets' who a few moments later can also be praised for behaving as they should. This will work in everyday situations such as the following:

**Example - A child pushing in a line**

A negative response would be to say 'Jack, for goodness sake, stop pushing!'

A positive response would be to say 'Robert, Sarah and Emma are standing very still in the line. Well done!' Then, if Jack stops pushing. 'Well done, Jack! You're standing beautifully as well, good boy!'

sticker'. Below are some types of rewards which are used:

- Social rewards - pleasant interactions such as a smile, praise, clapping, hugs.
- Activity rewards - having a go on the computer, choosing a song, choosing a story, playing a particular game.
- Token rewards - stars, stickers
- Material rewards - edible or usable items - such as a biscuit.

Discipline should be about positive re-enforcement of acceptable behaviour and positive role models. If a child is shouting and an adult responds by shouting at the child then the child will not understand that shouting is unacceptable.

> The adult's words and manner must be firm and leave the child in no doubt as to what will follow. Be fair, be clear, be consistent.
>
> 1 Gain attention
> 2 Say what the unwanted behaviour is
> 3 Say why the behaviour is unacceptable
> 4 State the action warranted by the behaviour
> 5 Give the instruction which implements the sanction

### Stronger action

Major incidents are fairly unusual. The most likely are bullying, either verbally or physically, name calling, or possible racist or sexist language. At pre-school level a child may hurt another child, for example, by biting, pinching, hitting, pulling hair or throwing sand or throwing a toy. In these situations stronger action is needed.

- Deal immediately with it - do not leave it until later.
- Avoid getting into battle with the child or a confrontational situation.
- Use the child's name but beware of giving the child a label.

**Example - All the children are listening to a story, a few start to fidget**

When a child is fidgeting instead of listening attentively, again praise for those who are listening is far more effective than constantly drawing attention to those who are not listening. The idea is to explicitly draw attention to the majority of children who are conforming to the acceptable norm.

**Example - At drinks time**

'Look how quietly these two tables are sitting' is much more likely to produce wanted behaviour from the third table, than 'Table three, you're the worst table in the room.'

In addition, it is important that the adult makes the desired behaviour clear. Telling children clearly what you want them to do is far more effective than telling them to stop doing something. 'John, stand still' is much clearer than 'John, stop running'. Children need to be told in language which they understand and are not confused by.

Distraction is also likely to produce the desired behaviour. If a child is picking her nose, for example, instead of saying 'Don't pick your nose!' say 'Wiggle your fingers'! As I'm sure you know, if children are told not to pick their noses, the automatic response appears to be to start picking again a moment later!

### Rewards

Where there is a specific behaviour which a child is struggling to achieve, rewards may be effective in the short-term. However, it is important not to over-rely on rewards. The adult has to remain in control and be the decision maker. For example, when a child has really made an effort and listened extremely well to the story (for him) he can be offered a reward. However, it is important that the adult is not bribed by the child, or does not put the child in control of the reward. For example, if the adult says, 'If you sit still you can have a star' then the child is in control. However, the adult could say, 'I may decide to give someone a star if someone sits beautifully.'

Alternatively, the adult may say nothing and observe the child closely. On spotting 'good behaviour' the adult will then reward the child and explain why. 'I saw you sharing that puzzle, well done, you can have a

*'Discipline should be about positive re-enforcement of acceptable behaviour and positive role models.'*

- Forgive and forget.

The child who has been attacked must be comforted and the child who is at fault helped to see the reason for adult intervention, without feeling attacked or undermined himself. In all circumstances children need to know the consequences of their misbehaviour. Use of consequences is an objective approach - if you spill the paint, you will wipe it up, if you drop your coat on the floor, you will pick it up. The adult's tone of voice can have a major impact on children's behaviour. There is a major difference between shouting and speaking firmly. 'Oh darling, please, you mustn't bite', in a kind and gentle tone of voice will not give the message that biting is unacceptable.

## Example 1
1 Jack

2 Throwing things

3 Can hurt people and

4 You will sit on the chair for a minute

5 And think about what you should have been doing.

In case of persistent misbehaviour adults can employ a warning procedure. Firstly, give a reminder of the rule: 'We do not throw sand'. Then a brief warning of the consequence: 'You will not play in the sand'. Then, if the behaviour persists, follow example 2.

## Example 2
1 Jessica

2 Throwing sand

3 Can hurt people

4 You will not play in the sand

5 Come and have a think about it.

If a major incident does occur which requires strong words or action, which may even make the child cry, it is a good idea to record it in a book. If a child tells a parent 'Mrs Jones got cross with me today', the parent may phone up wanting to know what's happened. It is professional to take the parent quietly to one side and explain the incident.

After an incident, if the child has the language, the adult should ask the child to tell him or her what caused the incident and ask 'What would be a better thing to do?' If the child then is spotted doing the right thing, this can be acknowledged with a comment such as 'Jack, I'm pleased to see you're taking turns. That's good - your mum will be pleased. Do you think you can keep it up? I think so.'

Other strategies include:

- Checking the physical setting - are they squabbling because there is not enough? Have they learned to share? Where is the adult?

- Changing the context - is it time to change the activity? Has the child been on the activity too long? Is it time to tidy away and get something different out?

- Providing help - for example, with a jigsaw puzzle thrown on the floor. Pick it up with the child and do it together.

- Changing the organisation - if the cars on the table are causing a problem, moving them onto the floor can diffuse the situation.

Whilst to say 'Come and sit on this chair and have a little think' may just help calm a situation, the use of a 'naughty' chair as a sanction is usually ineffective and not acceptable.

## Physical handling
The physical handling of children is a sensitive area. On rare occasions staff in groups can be accused of physical assault. The existence of a behaviour policy should clearly stipulate no use of corporal punishment or any other action which will frighten or humiliate a child. This would also include not only smacking but pinching, squeezing, hair pulling, isolation, putting a child in a cupboard or anything likely to cause emotional upset to the child. The adult must show that only 'reasonable physical restraint' was used to calm the situation and in particular to prevent the child from harming him or herself. For example, if a child was running towards a road or climbing over a fence and likely to fall, the adult would have no choice but to physically handle the child. Pre-school staff are probably in a less vulnerable position than Reception teachers as there is usually another adult around to witness the incident. If staff have attended relevant training courses and a comprehensive policy is in place, there are unlikely to be any problems.

A small minority of children do have emotional or behavioural difficulties which cause higher levels of concern. The parent should be consulted and perhaps seek advice from the health visitor, who in turn may recommend the support of an educational psychologist. Strategies available include the drawing up of detailed individual programmes, personal counselling, therapy or focused support.

In summary, then, children's behaviour is very complex but there are certain things that are known to encourage good behaviour. These are:

- clear rules

- praise

- showing correct behaviour

- consistency

- consequences

- preventing

- reinforcing good behaviour

## Acknowledgments
Some of the material for this section has been drawn from Solity J and Bull S (1987) *Classroom Management Principles to Practice* published by Croom Helm and Finch G *Handling Children's Behaviour* NCH Action For Children.

Caroline Jones, nursery owner and part-time lecturer at the University of Warwick

# Supporting children with learning difficulties

As more pre-school age children with special educational needs are being educated in mainstream settings, the need for information and practical ideas is becoming greater among early years professionals.

Assuming a child has no other primary cause of SEN, for example, hearing impairment, Down's syndrome or cerebral palsy, it is likely that learning difficulties will be the most common problem to become obvious at this stage.

There is no blueprint for supporting and managing children with learning difficulties. Each set of problems is as unique as the child himself. There are so many variables to be taken into account when planning a programme of work - his learning style, your teaching style, the amount of parental support, the available resources and equipment, the setting's SEN policy and so on - that each programme can be planned only by the people who will be implementing it for the child who will be using it.

Most early years professionals are excellent at identifying quickly a child who seems to be having learning difficulties. But a vague feeling that something is wrong has to be focused into specifics and then acted on. The first step in doing this is to decide whether the child:

■ scores poorly on assessment tests or profiles (whether standardised tests or the setting's own admission baseline assessments) in comparison with his peers;

■ has levels of development (in all or specific areas) and play that are noticeably lower than those of his peers;

■ makes little or no progress despite involvement in the nursery curriculum and fails to achieve the targets set;

■ makes little or no progress despite involvement in a differentiated curriculum.

If the child seems to meet all or most of these criteria, then action needs to be taken.

## Steps to follow after identifying concerns

1  Involve the child's parents. This is crucial (and a legal obligation) at all stages. A positive and active relationship with the child's parents is beneficial to everybody concerned.

2  Involve the Special Educational Needs Co-ordinator (SENCO).

3  Initiate Early Years Action with an Individual Education Plan (IEP), which should include the following points:

Child's name and date of birth
Date IEP implemented
Areas of difficulty
Two or three (no more!) areas of work and target dates
Teaching methods
Staff involved
Frequency of programme
Criteria for success
Equipment/apparatus
Date of next review

4  Review Early Years Action and the IEP about three months after implementation. If there are still concerns after two or three reviews, then

5  Initiate Early Years Action Plus, involving appropriate outside agents and specialist support. Review the IEP and plan a new one if necessary.

6  Review Early Years Action Plus and IEP. If there are still concerns after two or three reviews, the team will decide whether a statutory assessment is necessary.

## What's on a typical IEP?
**Name:** Joe Soap

**DOB:** 13.2.98

**IEP:** 18.9.01

**Areas of difficulty:** Joe has difficulty with

*'An IEP is not fixed in tablets of stone and can be changed if the targets are too difficult for the child. There's no failure in admitting that the IEP needs to be altered. The failure is in being too proud to change it and leaving the child to struggle.'*

early literacy and numeracy skills. He has no obvious physical or emotional problems.

**Targets to be reached by 18.12.01:**

■  Joe should be able to recognise his name from among others in his registration group.

■  Joe should be able to count from one to three using apparatus.

■  Joe should be able to recognise and name one, two and three when shown in written form.

**Teaching methods:** Initially in a one-to-one situation in the quiet corner, eventually moving into the main nursery areas to use counting displays, posters, name tags and so on.

**Staff involved:** Mrs Jones, nursery nurse; Mrs Smith, nursery nurse; Mrs Soap, mother, to work at home.

**Frequency of programme:** twice daily (morning and afternoon) for a maximum of ten minutes, five days per week.

**Criteria for success:**

◼ Joe can recognise his name from among a display of up to five others, four out of five times, in each session.

◼ Joe can count one, two or three items of apparatus correctly, four times out of five in each session.

◼ Joe can recognise and name one, two or three when shown in written form, four out of five times in each session.

**Equipment/apparatus:** name cards from Joe's registration group, cubes, counters, plastic sorting shapes, any appropriate counting apparatus of Joe's choice, paper, pencils and felt-tip pens.

**Date of next review:** 19.12.01

To be attended by Mrs Jones, Mrs Smith and Mrs Soap.

*(This is a fictional scenario. A sheet recording Joe's performance should be attached to the IEP.)*

## Working with the child on an Individual Education Plan (IEP)

◼ The record sheet designed by the setting should contain details of the dates that the child's performance was checked, by whom and with what result. Careful record-keeping is crucial.

◼ It is also essential to make a note of which areas are giving him difficulty.

◼ The Code of Practice recommends that the child's progress is reviewed every three months - it is important to keep an eye on him throughout that period.

◼ The IEP can be changed at any time.

◼ Be aware of the records of results - is a pattern emerging? For example, does Joe always fail to meet his targets in the same sessions?

◼ The teaching methods may play a part. For example, does Joe work better in a one-to-one situation? Is there a clash of personalities with Mrs Jones? Do his

sessions happen at a good time? Are the rewards and incentives offered to Joe sufficient to motivate him?

## Positive teaching methods are essential

◼ Always involve the child in his own record keeping. For example, allow him to put stickers on his chart or to choose

**Further reading:**

*Code of Practice on the Identification of Special Educational Needs* (DFE, 1994).

*Excellence for all Children - Meeting Special Educational Needs* (DfEE, 1997).

*SEN Code of Practice on the Identification and Assessment of Pupils with Special Educational Needs and SEN Thresholds: Good Practice Guidance on Identification and Provision for Pupils with Special Educational Needs* (consultation document) (DfEE, 2000).

*Handbook for Pre-School SEN Provision* Chris Spencer and Kate Schnelling (David Fulton, 1998).

*Special Needs in the Early Years* Sue Roffey (David Fulton, 1999).

which activity he wants to do as a reward for trying or achievement.

◼ Always work in small steps and don't overload the child. An IEP is not fixed in tablets of stone and can be changed if the targets are too difficult for the child. There's no failure in admitting that the IEP needs to be altered. The failure is in being too proud to change it and leaving the child to struggle.

◼ Always be patient. If it's a bad day and the child is driving you mad, take time away from each other and try again later when both of you feel calmer.

◼ Always be consistent in your approach. This is essential for the child to be able to learn and practise the skill being taught.

◼ Always give the child plenty of repetition. He'll need lots of practice and help, so don't be afraid of 'overkill'. If possible, though, try to offer different activities to consolidate the skill.

◼ Always praise the child whenever he

achieves success and always refer to failure in a positive way. For example, 'That was a really good try, Joe. Let's see if you can make it this time by doing ... '

◼ Always be prepared to be flexible. If it takes standing on your head to get a point across, then do it!

◼ Always check previous achievements on a regular basis. Skills that were taught some weeks beforehand may need to be revisited and consolidated again! Don't assume that when a target has been achieved that's the end - keep checking.

◼ Always remember the child is not here for the professional - the professional is here for the child!

Collette Drifte is a writer, lecturer, INSET provider and consultant on special educational needs and early years education.

# Identifying and **supporting** more able **children**

In Africa there is a saying: 'When you plant a tree, never plant only one. Plant three – one for shade, one for fruit and one for beauty.' This may also be sound educational advice. In a world where there would appear to be increasing pressure to excel, it may be that practitioners are planting only one tree – we see children in terms of their ability to be 'fruitful' or 'achieve' school targets.

With the advent of Early Intervention and the publication of documents such as the *Curriculum Guidance for the Foundation Stage* and *Curriculum Framework for Children 3-5*, we are becoming more and more aware of children who might be called 'intelligent', 'bright' or 'more able'. Identifying some of these children will be easy – 'I can read that book myself' – but I would suggest that being more able is more than just being able to read, write and count ahead of what might be expected.

## What does it mean to be more able?

Each of you will have your own ideas about what it means to be more able. The language we use, our personal experiences, the media and culture we experience, will all have shaped our concept of what a more able child can do.

Our ideas influence what we believe children are capable of. For example, do you believe intelligence is fixed? If you do, then this is likely to mean that you will not believe a child is capable of growing and improving. If a child believes this, then they will give up when they fail, believing that they can't get any better – 'I'm not clever enough'. On the other hand, if you think that problems are to be solved then you will believe that intelligence is not fixed but able to grow – 'I can improve if I practice' – and children, too, will begin to think this way.

Another topic worth exploring as a staff is in which areas of the curriculum are children most likely to be identified as more able. Miss X, the key practitioner in the pre-school setting, may think it's about abilities in a range of curricular areas. Mr Y in Reception class or primary one may think it's about maths and language. Mrs Z, as the head, may think it includes aesthetic subjects – music, drama, art, PE. These different perceptions will influence how they present the curriculum. Coming to some kind of shared understanding about what intelligence is and how it is demonstrated will help to establish that everyone is working towards the same goal. It will also help to make sure that you recognise, celebrate and value a range of abilities. The first step for any setting may be to decide what they understand by the word 'intelligence' and what abilities constitute a child being identified as more able.

### Pointers

There are a number of pointers that might lead us to think a child is more able. They may, for example:

■ show advanced development in the area of thinking skills – they are imaginative and creative, they can read, write and use numbers in a well-developed way;

■ display a definite learning style – they are motivated and inquisitive, they can work independently, they have good concentration;

■ have highly developed speech and language skills – they can use metaphors, carry out instructions, have a good vocabulary;

■ develop early motor skills - they know left and right, they can complete difficult puzzles/jigsaws, they can take apart and rebuild objects;

■ demonstrate well-constructed social skills – they have an understanding of the rules, an ability to form close friendships or an interest in social topics.

As with any check-lists there will be children who don't fall into these categories. Stereotypes about more able or intelligent children can blind practitioners to children who do not fit traditional ideas. So, check-lists can be helpful, but only if used with caution!

We know that high quality early education is vital to children's development. If we are going to enhance learning, we need to build on prior learning. If children are displaying certain abilities then we need to find out what those are and then challenge them. Going through every stepping stone in order to get to the end may not be helpful and will certainly not be challenging to young enquiring minds.

Underachievement can be the result where lack of challenge prevails; this has to be avoided.

## Types of intelligence

Having agreed that we should be catering for children who demonstrate abilities, I would suggest that the question practitioners need to be asking is not 'How smart are you?' but 'How are you smart?' Answering this question will naturally move us away from traditional views that intelligence is narrowly based on maths and language abilities and towards a wider approach where a variety of abilities are included. Howard Gardner (1983) suggests that there are eight intelligences:

- Word smart
- Maths smart
- Music smart
- People smart
- Self smart
- Body smart
- Picture smart
- Nature smart

We all have at least three areas of strength from this list. Profiling the children with whom we work across the seven intelligences will produce jagged results. This will allow us to see where we need to continue to challenge, but it will also allow us to see where we need to develop certain skills. If children enter settings with a range of abilities which are not challenged then the result may be underachievement.

Offering a curriculum for young able learners may prove to be challenging. We have to acknowledge that they need the same kind of demanding activities that older children require but at the same time be age appropriate. 'More of the same' is not a helpful strategy. However, too difficult a task may also result in boredom. Our understanding of the child and his or her abilities is crucial if just the right amount of challenge is to be offered. More able children will often crave an intellectual peer with whom they can share their thoughts and ideas. When this happens children will often seek out adults in the setting. The adult has to ensure that they don't simply give the child answers whilst at the same time meeting the needs of all the other children in their care. As I said, a challenging task!

There seems to be a general concern about the effects of 'hot housing' children or indeed of labelling them: 'too much too soon'; 'we'll turn them off'; 'they'll not have any friends'. Whilst too much too soon can indeed be damaging, it is perhaps not so much that the children have been identified that creates the problem but more the misuse of the information we receive that can lead to difficulties. It is therefore vital that we plan a curriculum that acknowledges and values abilities, wherever these may lie.

Play is a wonderful way of offering learning experiences. Young children play naturally and derive enjoyment from the experience. We must therefore consider what the child will gain from the play experiences we are providing. Young able children, and indeed all children, should be involved in planning their curriculum. This encourages responsibility for their own learning and increases motivation. Young able children can be capable of working on their own. However, because they can 'get on with things' they are often left to do so with very little interaction with more knowledgeable others. It is important to ensure that any interaction between the adult and the child is of a high quality. Planning this interaction is vital.

## Interaction with adults

Given that time is always of the essence we should consider the role we will embrace during the interaction. Will we be giving instructions? Will we be assessing? Will we be posing questions? Care should also be given to the way in which we respond. Are we creating an atmosphere of trust and mutual respect?

Of course, these suggestions are good for all children. However, some activities will seek to offer children broader and deeper learning experiences through open-ended tasks, abstract concepts, complex ideas or the teaching of thinking skills. As has been noted by Callahan (1996), 'It is extremely difficult to build a strong differentiated curriculum on a weak basic curriculum'. It is therefore important to establish that you are offering a strong basic curriculum before developing strategies for young able children.

If we concentrate on only one area of development and we see children in terms of their ability to be fruitful or achieve, we may be planting only one tree. On the other hand, by valuing and celebrating a range of abilities, we will help to make sure that we are planting three trees – one for shade, one for fruit and one for beauty.

Margaret Sutherland, lecturer,
Faculty of Education, Glasgow University.

# Working with an **autistic** child

Take a moment to imagine what it would be like to live in a world where words, gestures, facial expressions and displays of emotion mean almost nothing to you. This is the isolating experience of more than 500,000 families in Britain whose lives are touched by autism.

## What is autism?

Autism affects the way a person communicates and relates to people around them. The term autistic spectrum is often used because the condition varies; some people may have accompanying learning disabilities while others are more able, with average or above average intelligence.

Asperger syndrome is at the more able end of the spectrum while Kanner syndrome, sometimes referred to as classic autism, is at the less able end. However, despite wide-ranging differences, everyone with the condition has difficulty with social interaction, social communication and imagination.

## Early signs

Parents are astute judges of their child's development and most often it is they who notice that 'something is not right', usually when their child is around two to three years old.

Distressingly, in some cases a child may seem to be developing quite normally and then suddenly appears to start losing the skills that he or she has acquired.

The signs of autism are varied. Parents and carers might notice that their child takes no interest in creative or imaginative play, preferring to repeat the same activity time and time again. Perhaps they find that their child repeats actions or words, behaves in public in ways that are odd or inappropriate, fails to make eye contact or has an almost obsessional interest in a particular subject or object - it has not been unknown for children to become fascinated by household appliances like vacuum cleaners!

In addition, a child with autism may become very distressed if routines are altered - for example, if mum varies the usual walk to the shops, or decides to serve the evening meal at a different time.

Relationships can be difficult and not only for parents. Children with autism can sometimes appear to be disruptive, rude and indifferent to other youngsters when playing or socialising. Occasionally their behaviour in public can be misunderstood by onlookers as a display of temper or naughtiness - the resulting comments made can be distressing and hurtful for parents who are doing their best to cope in a difficult situation.

## Diagnosis

Early diagnosis is vital to ensure that the child and family receive support and educational guidance as soon as possible as this can have a positive impact on the future.

Most parents who suspect something is wrong approach their GP. They may also contact their local education authority to ask for an assessment of their child's needs. However, although awareness of autism is increasing, some families still experience frustrating delays before their suspicions are finally confirmed and a diagnosis obtained. (Occasionally, some of the more able children with autism, including those with Asperger syndrome, are not diagnosed until they are in their mid to late teens - sometimes even later.)

## Support for parents

Once a firm diagnosis is obtained, a prime question for parents is education. A key aim is to overcome or reduce the disabling effects of autism by providing a broad and relevant curriculum and giving extra help in the areas of communication and social skills as well as compensating for difficulties in imagination.

In the nursery or pre-school situation an autistic child will need specialised assistance targeting these areas and to help them cope with the school environment generally. It is accepted that early intervention can make a real difference to the life of both the child and their family.

The National Autistic Society has a project known as EarlyBird which aims to support parents in the period between diagnosis and school placement. As part of the project, therapists work with parents to establish good practice in applying a knowledge of autism. They are shown techniques to put them in control of their child's development at an early age, to help pre-empt inappropriate behaviours and realise their child's potential.

# General points to bear in mind

Remember that you are trying to improve the quality of life for the child, helping him or her to behave in a more socially acceptable way so that others respond better and so that the child is happier.

- Make sure that the day is predictable and safe by establishing meaningful routines. Children with autism learn best through practical activities that are meaningful to them, for example routines for putting on clothing, eating, play.

- Keep calm and avoid using a raised excited voice. Use gentle, slow movements with frequent smiles and touches.

- Language - keep it simple, often backed up with photographs, pictures, body language, gesture and facial expressions.

- For any child with autism, learning to communicate about the things that are important to them is the best place to start.

- When trying to work with an autistic child get down to their level by sitting or kneeling on the floor, or for a more structured approach use a small table with a chair at the right height.

- For young children with autism a key aim is to help them enjoy exploring their own lips, tongue and teeth and the sounds they can make. It is important to make any play with sounds fun.

- Encourage children to join in with 'turn taking' play using sounds. This is a way of practising conversation as well as practising speech sounds.

- Encourage words - but don't worry if they don't sound quite right to begin with.

- The play of children with autism is often taken over by their need for 'sameness'. Play becomes another sort of repetitive activity which can block other people out. Try to encourage variety in the child's play so that new experience and learning is made possible.

- Children with autism also need to learn how to play with people. They need to learn that people can be interesting and fun. Again this opens up a whole range of new experiences and opportunities to learn.

- Keep a watchful eye to ensure that the child is not teased or bullied.

## Helpful approaches

Early years workers who care for a child with autism should be aware of several helpful approaches.

**Visually interesting toys/activities:** Children with autistic spectrum disorders tend to prefer toys that involve visuo spatial skills such as shape and colour matching, jigsaw puzzles or constructional materials. Examples include: bubble blowers, torches, shape and colour matching toys, jigsaws, pop-up toys, construction toys, train toys, drawing, colouring and painting, books with flaps, touch and feel books, puzzle books and videos.

**Physical activity:** It is useful to encourage physical activities that are enjoyable without the need for imagination or understanding and use of language. Physical exercise is reported to diminish inappropriate behaviour and such activities are also helpful for improving motor co-ordination. Many children love 'rough and tumble' play which helps them develop eye contact and social interaction. Examples include: swings, slides, musical toys, water toys, rocking horses, trampolines, climbing frames, ride-on toys, paddling pools, sand pits.

**Games to play with other people:** Try to engage the children in simple games. Dancing games such as 'The Hokey Cokey' involve others and have consistent rules. Children can pick up and enjoy the routine of these activities. Other examples include: singing and dancing games, pass the parcel, peek-a-boo, 'Round and round the garden', simple picture/lotto games, snap, skittles, and catch the ball games.

## Appropriate provision

As a spectrum disorder, autism demands a flexible response and in practical terms a range of provision is needed. Many authorities aim for all children with special needs to be taught within their local mainstream schools. This gives the children a chance to become integrated into society with non-disabled peers and offers the possibility of making friends close to home.

For some children with autism mainstream education is both appropriate and desirable. With the support and advice of knowledgeable professionals it can be adapted to meet individual needs. For other children, however, the mainstream environment can be terrifying and confusing with things appearing to happen at random and in unexpected ways. This leads to great distress for the child and disruption for the school.

While excellent, high quality specialist education for children with autism exists in the UK, sadly there are too few places and parents often have to struggle to find the right place for their child. Sometimes their choice is limited or the place they eventually find is many miles from home.

The National Autistic Society (NAS) has been at the leading edge of devising appropriate programmes and runs schools for children whose abilities cover the full range of the autistic spectrum. Day and residential options offer flexible responses to the needs of each child and their family.

Kate Griffin, National Autistic Society.

## Where to go for help

A first point of contact for parents and carers seeking advice or information is the NAS's Autism Helpline, a written and telephone enquiry service. The phone line is open between 10am - 11.30am and 2pm - 3.30pm weekdays.
Telephone: 0207 903 3555.

Professionals may be interested in the society's information centre which provides advice and information for students, researchers, teachers and members of the public with an interest in autism (Telephone: 0207 903 3599).
The society's publications department offers a wide range of helpful literature.

For more information, write to the National Autistic Society, 393 City Road, London EC1V 1NE.

# Meeting the needs of the **visually impaired** child

**The Code of Practice includes the principle that, wherever possible (and subject to parental views) children with special educational needs should be educated in mainstream settings. This includes the education of the under-fives and so we can expect to see visually impaired children in our nurseries and Reception classes.**

## What do we mean by visual impairment?

Visual impairment (VI) refers to those children who have difficulties in seeing which call for the use of special educational methods and adaptations to materials and who need to use specialist aids and equipment for learning. (For example, the use of low vision aids - magnifying glasses, CCTV, large print and Braille.) The term covers those children who are blind or partially sighted but not children who wear glasses. For common eye conditions such as myopia (short-sightedness), hypermetropia (long-sightedness) or astigmatism (where the eye focuses unevenly and objects are seen as blurred and distorted) then a child's vision will be corrected through wearing glasses.

Children with a VI, though, are not a heterogenous group. The children will have a range of personalities, interests and abilities as well as a range of types and degree of VI, from relatively slight loss through more severe degrees of loss to total blindness. For example, a child may experience one or more of the following:

- ❏ Have only light perception
- ❏ Have a blurred view of the world
- ❏ Have only central vision and no peripheral vision (tunnel vision)
- ❏ No central vision and therefore difficulty with colour and fine detail
- ❏ Pain and distress caused by bright lights

Approximately 1 in 2,000 children is visually impaired. Yet children with total blindness form less than 20 per cent of the total population of children with a VI. The other 80 per cent may be registered blind but will have some useful vision. While this remaining vision may not always be very helpful to an elderly person, it has enormous significance for children who

may benefit from training in interpreting the incomplete or imperfect images they see. Whatever the level of VI the child should *always* be encouraged to use their vision. Little vision does not deteriorate with use.

Specialist advisors or peripatetic teachers will support most VI children who are educated alongside their sighted peers. It will be the responsibility of this teacher to ensure that you and your colleagues feel confident in working with the child by providing practical support and advice. Parents, too, should be involved in the education of their child and can offer valuable advice on the child's specific VI, the level of their sight, what tasks present difficulties and the possible implications for learning.

## Symptoms to look out for

Many of you will not have a child with a VI in your setting at the moment. However, in the course of your work you may be concerned about a particular child. What then are the possible symptoms of a VI, which may require further assessment? The list below is not exhaustive and a child may not display all the symptoms. Similarly, a child may have some of the symptoms but investigations show that they are not caused by a VI. If in doubt, observe the child over a period of time and doing a variety of tasks. Discussion with the parents should then be the first step before contacting the local education authority's advisory service for VI.

### Head position
- Child moves head rather than eyes when

concentrating on visual tasks
- Frequent nodding of head when concentrating on visual tasks
- Head tilts in what appears to be an uncomfortable position

### Eye position
- Frowning or squinting when looking at pictures/books
- Aversion to bright lights
- Eyelids are drooping or swollen
- Unusual eye movements, including a rapid involuntary movement (nystagmus)
- Excessive blinking/rubbing of eyes
- Crossed eyes
- Closing or covering one eye when playing or working

### Movement
- When walking, displays an unusual, very short or very long length of stride
- Poor posture
- Clumsy movements, particularly prone to bumping into objects at side or at feet

- Fear of heights
- Poor balance

**Behaviour**
- Not answering questions unless asked by name
- Short attention span in visual tasks
- Fumbling over fine hand-eye co-ordination tasks
- Reluctance to join in outdoor activities

## Effects of a VI on development

During infancy the sighted child accomplishes vast progress. They move from being egocentric to interacting sociably with peers and adults. Their language moves from babble to well constructed sentences. Their motor development moves from them having little control to that of a two-year-old who has relatively good gross motor control and is developing fine motor control. A sighted physically able child in their first few years of life seems to learn without effort - vision plays a vital role, providing a continuous, rich, consistent, precise and reliable source of information to help the child orientate to and identify objects and people.

A visual impairment imposes many restrictions on a child's ability to learn since the majority of our learning is visually based. The effects of a VI may be seen in three ways:

**1. Experiences** will be limited in range and variety - a child who does not see or sees incompletely will have a reduced ability to learn by imitation; a child who doesn't observe an activity won't attempt it for himself.

**2. Movement** may be curtailed - if there is an inability to see their surroundings, the child will be less motivated to reach out or crawl. For security the child may tend to stay in one place, thereby restricting their range of movements.

**3. Control of their environment** and self in relation to the environment is restricted. There may be a delay in bonding between mother and child due to a lack of eye contact and whereas a sighted child may smile in order to be picked up and cuddled this is lacking in a VI child. Understanding body awareness and knowing where they are in space is also hindered.

A child's play requirements will depend very much on their level of vision and visual defect. Unlike a sighted child who can use their eyes to observe the environment, a VI child will need the environment to come to them. It isn't true that the VI child will have better hearing or tactile skills and so pre-school or nursery staff must help him use these senses and make sense of a bewildering world.

## How you can support the child

The five points listed here are not exhaustive but should provide a useful starting point for appropriately meeting the child's needs within the early years environment. The benefits of such a framework should in fact meet the needs of all children and not just the VI child, helping them all to make the transition between home and pre-school, between the familiar and the unfamiliar and from dependence to independence.

## Partnership with parents

Nursery or pre-school may be the first time the child has left the familiarity of home for any length of time without their parents. Staff must recognise that parents know their child better than they do. The visual functioning of many VI children may vary during the day and according to their general health - it is very demanding to use impaired vision. Therefore ask the parents:

- About visual impairment.

- What is their level of sight?

- When does the child become tired?

- What tasks do they enjoy/find difficult?

- Does he wear glasses - if yes, does he also have a tinted pair?

Explain the pre-school routine carefully to parents and expect them to ask you questions. They will need this information to prepare their child.

## The learning environment
### Visual environment:
The lighting and decor within your setting can both hinder or help learning. Lighting does not mean bright lights - some eye conditions require lower than normal lighting levels. Blinds/curtains may be needed to prevent hard shadow and glare.

Think about the child's seating position at circle time. Do not sit/stand in front of a window - the light may cause discomfort for the child and your facial expressions will be lost. Consider contrast within your setting - contrast between floors-walls-skirting boards, between doors and door handles (perhaps paint handles black so they are easily located). Display boards should be bright and clear and used to break up large expanses of wall. The use of colour and contrast may also enhance safety - place a dark rug on a light carpet to alert the child to the location of a piece of furniture. Provide contrasting table mats and cups to reduce spillage.

**Sound environment:**

All VI children will need to use information from what they hear rather more than sighted children. The sound environment should provide information to help a child understand what is happening around them and to help with orientation. Special sound clues could be introduced:

■ Chimebells on the door so a child knows when someone is coming in/out.

■ A whistle to signify tidy-up time.

■ Goodbye song at the end of the nursery session.

As a VI child does not automatically hear better he will need to be encouraged to listen (for example, through turn taking games/sound lotto games).

**Tactile environment:**

The layout and organisation of the room is important. It needs to be familiar to the VI child. More than one visit prior to starting will be necessary. Actively introduce the child to the environment, telling them where they are by using landmarks. For example, talk about the rough mat by the door, the change in surface from concrete to grass when you are nearing the slide. Spend these visits, too, observing the child to see how he copes in different situations and to observe their exploratory techniques. Remember, a

sighted child can continually gaze around and will gradually absorb his new surroundings, the VI child can't.

Once the child has joined your group, don't expect too much from him at first. If he is reluctant to move around then provide a 'safe corner', where he is allowed the time to explore and discover just a small space. Once he is more confident he can be encouraged to explore the wider environment.

The setting should be organised into defined areas: creative corner, building area and so on. Materials relating to each area should be clearly labelled and the VI child should be given plenty of opportunity to explore and handle the objects. Keep the layout the same so he can build up a visual memory of the room and develop independence.

## Presentation of tasks

This is a key issue for all children. When introducing new activities/tasks always start by using established routines and then do

something new. The child must be actively introduced to environment information, for example:

■ Activity areas - does the child know where they are?

■ Circle time - has the child been sat in the best place to maximise visual input? Has he been shown how to do the action/finger rhymes?

■ Art activities - wherever possible have a finished product so he knows what is expected.

■ Snack-time - have you explained where the biscuits are kept and the milk is poured from a jug?

For close work (jigsaws, writing, threading) there should be a clear visual or physical edge to the work area so the child can easily locate the things he is using.

Where possible, toys/resources should be bold, bright and contrasting (remember - BBC). For totally blind children sound provides the only motivation to reach out and explore so sound making toys or ones with movable parts are essential. Toys may need to be anchored within easy reach until the child has learned to search for and find them. Encourage all VI children to use both their hands, telling them what they are touching and how toys work. In this way they will begin to understand what objects are, what they do and what they feel like.

*'A sighted physically able child in their first few years of life seems to learn without effort - vision plays a vital role, providing a continuous, rich, consistent, precise and reliable source of information to help the child orientate to and identify objects and people. A visual impairment imposes many restrictions on a child's ability to learn since the majority of our learning is visually based.'*

## Experiences

Children with a VI need access to first-hand experiences wherever possible. Best (1992 p74) says:

'They should not have to rely solely on descriptions given by other people of situations they cannot see clearly. These descriptions will not be as full or meaningful as first-hand experiences, will place additional demands on the child's memory . . . and may remove some of the active involvement in learning through experiences'.

Only later in life will the VI child be able to connect the miniatures in their mind with their full size counterparts and so it is important that they handle and talk about as many manageable real things as possible. For example:

- Before setting up a laundry in the home corner visit a real laundry.

- Initially use real cups and saucers in the home corner alongside the play ones to help with association.

- Use a variety of natural objects wherever possible.

- Good quality photographs are better than cartoon pictures and do not distort a child's perception of objects.

- Think about nursery songs - does the child know what a pail is? ('Jack and Jill') Or what a spout is? ('Incy Wincy Spider').

## Communication

Language is an important means for getting acquainted and sharing experiences with any child. Before the sighted child begins to speak, he is able to communicate using a number of ways. They acknowledge our presence, express preferences with a smile or a frown and understand our displeasure when we frown or can interpret our blank stares when we don't understand what they are trying to say! These non-verbal signals are completely/partly absent with a VI child who is dependent on verbal communication and physical contact. Staff will need to adopt the following strategies:

- Provide a running commentary on the world (but don't talk non-stop!) Identify objects, describe movement, for example 'I'm lifting you into the air'.

- Use relevant situational language: 'We're going into the kitchen to get the drinks tray'. In this way the child will begin to connect experiences with the words that describe them.

- At the start of new activities explain what is happening - don't assume the child will have picked up on visual clues.

- Always start a sentence with the child's name so the child knows you are talking to him.

- Always tell the child when you are approaching/leaving.

Keeva Austin, formerly manager of the Early Years Assessment Centre, Exhall Grange Special School, Coventry.

## Useful addresses

RNIB, 105 Judd Street, London WC1H 9NE
Tel: 0207 388 1266
www.rnib.org.uk

Social services - many have special social workers for people with impaired vision (rehabilitation workers).

LOOK - part of the National Federation of Families with VI Children, Queen Alexandra College, 49 Court Oak Road, Harborne, Birmingham.
B17 9TG
Tel: 0121 428 5038
www.look-uk.org

Partially Sighted Society, Queen's Road, Doncaster DN1 2NX.
Tel: 01302 323132

# Helping children
# who are deaf

There are about 28,000 children in the UK with permanent deafness ranging from moderate to profound. Other children will have mild deafness and some will have a deafness that affects one ear only (unilateral deafness). Other commonly used terms to describe different types and levels of deafness are hearing loss, hard of hearing, partially deaf/hearing or hearing-impaired. Many more children will experience temporary deafness, which can be caused by glue ear. This can affect around 80 per cent of children during some stage in their childhood, so it is important that staff who work in early years settings have some knowledge of deafness so that they know how to support deaf children and their parents.

There are two main types of deafness: conductive and sensori-neural.

**Conductive deafness** is the most common type. Basically it means that sounds cannot pass efficiently through the outer and middle ear to the cochlea and auditory nerve. This is often caused by fluid in the middle ear (glue ear) and sometimes blockages such as wax in the ear canal.

**Sensori-neural deafness**, or nerve deafness as it is sometimes called, usually means that the cochlea is not processing the sound effectively. Often the cause of sensori-neural deafness is not known, but there are often hereditary factors. Deafness may be passed down in families even if there is no apparent history of deafness. Deafness can also be caused by an infectious disease such as rubella, mumps, measles or meningitis. A child may become deaf because of a shortage of oxygen in the bloodstream at birth or some other birth trauma. It is also known that premature babies are more at risk of being deaf.

When a child experiences both of these types of deafness it is often referred to as 'mixed deafness'. Few children are totally deaf. Most children will have some hearing at some frequencies.

## Advice for parents
Parents who are worried about their child's level of hearing should contact their family doctor (GP) and/or health visitor (HV) and ask for a hearing assessment. The GP can examine the child's ears for any signs of infection and may prescribe a course of antibiotics, if appropriate. Some health centres can provide a hearing assessment.

Parents can, if necessary, request a referral to the ear, nose and throat (ENT) clinic or audiology department at their local hospital if they are concerned about their child's hearing and want further investigations to be carried out.

## What is glue ear?
Glue ear is one of the most common childhood conditions. Children under the age of five are the largest group affected. It is a build-up of mucus or fluid within the middle ear, often associated with colds and coughs. In adults and older children any fluid produced by the cells lining the middle ear usually drains away through the Eustachian tube, which runs from the middle ear to the back of the throat. In children this tube is not as vertical and wide as it will be when they get older and as a result doesn't work as well. Glue ear is often, but not always linked with ear infections.

### Treatment for glue ear
Many children may experience glue ear following a cold, which can clear without any treatment. Sometimes a course of antibiotics may be prescribed if there is any pain or sign of infection. For some children with persistent glue ear, an operation may be needed to drain the fluid from the middle ear. This involves inserting a ventilation tube called a grommet into the eardrum. This is a common treatment for glue ear and improves the hearing whilst the grommet is in place. Grommets usually stay in the eardrum until it heals and pushes the grommet out. Though an effective treatment for many children, sometimes the fluid comes back and another grommet operation may be considered.

### Temporary deafness
Glue ear can sometimes develop unnoticed. Changes in behaviour, becoming tired and frustrated, lack of concentration, preferring to play alone and not responding when called may indicate glue ear. These signs can often be mistaken for stubbornness, rudeness and being naughty. Reduced hearing can make understanding conversation difficult and cause a delay in a child's speech and language development. A child with temporary deafness would still be able to hear many sounds and would generally be aware of sounds around the home. However, speech is made up of sounds with different pitches and different loudness levels that can become difficult to hear with background noise. Young children at an early stage in their language development, if affected by deafness, will have difficulty hearing all the different speech sounds and this will affect their understanding of speech, and the way they speak.

## Hearing aids
There are many different types of hearing aids, some of which can transmit sounds to the ear in different ways. All hearing aids (with the exception of cochlear implants) have a common purpose - to amplify sound. They come in various shapes and types. Most are worn behind the ear, though some are worn on the body or in the ear. Some hearing aids, such as bone-anchored hearing aids and cochlear implants, have parts that are surgically implanted into the ear. Cochlear implants, instead of amplifying sound, send electrical signals directly to the auditory nerve. The implant bypasses the damaged hair cells in the cochlea (that cannot be stimulated by conventional hearing aids) to provide a sensation of hearing.

## Communication and language
The ability to develop good communication skills will help a deaf child to build up confidence to communicate with others and in turn will help them to develop emotional, personal and social skills. It is also how they learn about and understand

the world around them. There are a number of factors that can help to make it easier for a deaf child to develop good communication and language skills. These include:

• the early and accurate identification of deafness
• the family having access to clear, balanced information, advice and support
• where appropriate, access to technology such as hearing aids to make the best use of residual hearing
• positive acceptance, support and commitment from the family
• the child and family having the opportunity to learn about deaf awareness and other deaf issues

There is a range of communication options available to deaf children and their families. All deaf children have different needs, so the way in which they communicate will vary. Pre-school children will either be encouraged to develop their speech and language skills through spoken English or through sign language or a mixture of both.

Many parents will want their child to learn to speak. However, some parents might decide, either soon after their child has been identified as deaf or when it becomes obvious that their child is struggling to acquire spoken language, to introduce sign language. They will use signs taken from British Sign Language, a visual language using handshapes, facial expressions, gestures and body language to communicate. It has a structure and grammar different from that of written and spoken English. Sign Supported English uses BSL signs but in English word order. Many parents may use this at first and develop their BSL skills at a later stage to coincide with their child's language acquisition.

If a parent decides not to use sign language they will most probably use one of the auditory-oral approaches which maintains that with the use of hearing aids, cochlear implants and radio aids to amplify residual hearing, children can develop their listening skills and so a spoken language. The most widely used of this approach is the natural aural approach.

A child will use one of three main communication options when they attend school. These are: auditory-oral approach, sign bilingualism, and total communication (TC).

## Communicating with a deaf child
• Make sure you have a child's attention before starting to sign or speak to them.
• Make sure there is good lighting so that your face is not in a shadow and the child can read your facial expressions and/or lipread.
• Make sure that you are facing the child and maintaining good eye contact. Don't sit too close. For lipreading and signing purposes the best distance is between 1 and 2 metres.
• Speak clearly, naturally and at a normal pace (speaking too slowly or shouting will distort lip patterns).
• Try to make sure that background noise is kept to a minimum. Children who use hearing aids/cochlear implants or children with mild or unilateral deafness will find it particularly difficult to pick out what is being said.

## Teachers of the deaf
Very soon after a child has been identified with a permanent deafness, the family are contacted by a teacher of the deaf (often a peripatetic). Their role will be to support a child's development of language and communication skills. This will be the same whether they use oral skills, such as speech and lipreading, sign language or a combination of both of these. If appropriate, they can also support a child within a mainstream setting.

The pre-school period is a critical time for acquiring good speech and language skills. There is a constant need for repetition of speech sounds to give them adequate experience of speech and the ability to associate speech with meaning.

## Technology in the classroom
Equipment such as a soundfield system is a good way of improving acoustic conditions in the classroom for all children. This system includes a microphone, worn by the teacher, which is connected to an amplifier. Loudspeakers are fitted around the classroom, often on the walls or ceiling. Radio aids are used to help make listening

in the classroom easier for children using hearing aids or cochlear implants. The teacher wears the transmitter with a microphone. The sounds are then transmitted by radio waves to the receiver, which is worn by the child. A radio aid helps to reduce the background noise and helps a child to concentrate on one person's voice, ie the teacher.

The National Deaf Children's Society loans out radio aids and other environmental aids for children and families to try out at home and in school. If you would like more details of the Blue Peter Loan service, or any other aspect of technology, please contact the Technology Service Team at the NDCS.

# Including the child with **cerebral palsy**

**From the moment of birth, or soon after, children with cerebral palsy (cp) have very different learning experiences from their able bodied peers.**

Babies experience a short, frustrating period of helplessness quickly followed by an increasingly active exploration of their world. They experience their world through lying, sitting, reaching, rolling, crawling and standing. In a few months they are up and away. Babies born with cp do not explore their world independently at the same times as their peers, if at all. Many, in addition to the physical difficulties, also have an altered perception of space and altered sensations of touch. The picture they build of their world may well be a very different one to others of their age.

When a small child with cp joins a pre-school group where staff have little or no previous experience to draw on staff will be unsure of their ground. They should be reassured that their experience of working with and understanding the needs of a broad range of children will stand them in good stead. However, it is important for staff to have a basic understanding of what cp is and how it affects children.

## What is cerebral palsy?
Cp is caused by abnormalities in the brain usually before, during or soon after, birth. Fifteen hundred babies are affected each year, roughly one in 400 children in the UK. Cp is not infectious and, although the disability may become more noticeable with age, it is not progressive. Cerebral palsy jumbles up the messages going from the brain to the muscles causing them to behave oddly. There are three types of cerebral palsy corresponding to the three areas of the brain that can be affected.

The first is spastic cp which occurs when the part of the brain controlling thought, movement and sensation is affected. 'Spastic' means 'stiff' and the stiffness can affect the arms and legs and possibly the neck and trunk. The terms quadriplegia (four limbs), diplegia (both legs) and hemiplegia (one side) are used to describe this type of cp. The muscles are very tight and limbs get pulled out of line.

The second type, athetoid cp, results in children having floppy muscles and uncontrolled movements of their legs and arms. When messages are sent to move muscles the floppiness can rapidly become tightness causing the limb to fly outwards. Children may also have difficulty with the fine movements of the mouth and tongue, causing problems with speech, chewing and swallowing.

The third type, ataxic cp, causes shaky jerky movements and particularly affects fine motor control. Children with ataxia may also be unsteady when walking.

Children may have some effects and not others. Some children are only mildly affected while others are profoundly affected. Some may experience two, or all three, types of cp. There is no treatment or cure but some of the effects can be helped by therapy and teaching. Because the muscles pull abnormally they can cause the child to sit or lie in odd ways which can result in stiffness and pain. Correct positioning in sitting, standing or lying can go a long way to helping prevent pain and can really make a difference to helping the child get involved in learning.

Four out of ten babies born with cerebral palsy have other difficulties. Some children have great difficulty unscrambling the messages they receive from their eyes. In the most severe cases children may appear blind but more commonly will have difficulty making sense of pictures or writing.

## Spatial awareness

Many children have difficulty with spatial awareness. If they are walking or moving their own wheelchair they bump into things; they cannot judge the speed of cars when crossing the road. In the group they may find it difficult to judge how much space they need and may 'push in'. Commonly they find it difficult to hold the picture of an object in their head with consequences for copying and mathematics.

## Hearing difficulties

Hearing difficulties are commonly associated with the athetoid form of cp but colds and glue ear affect all children. Many children are sensitive to sounds and startle at loud noises. Usually they become more tolerant of noise as they become used to the group.

## Speech problems

Speech problems are common. Speech and language therapists will suggest the best way to help the child communicate and also help with chewing or swallowing problems. Most children will use speech to communicate but some will need an alternative form either to help them make their meaning clear or as their best way of talking. If children get speech aids early it can help reduce frustration. Speech aids might come in the form of a picture book or symbols, like little cartoons, that the child points to in order to clarify meaning. For some children the speech aid will be in the form of a speech synthesiser with pre-recorded messages activated by pressing switches. Using a speech aid will never prevent speech and it can help the child take part in group work and shout out with the others. Speech and language therapists will recommend what the individual child needs.

*'It is vital that staff other than the child's support assistant become confident in handling, positioning and communicating with the child. A child may visit the group without this happening, a child may be made welcome, but for the child to be included everyone has to feel confident.'*

## Epilepsy

Epilepsy is the additional problem most commonly associated with cp and is usually easily controlled. The medicines may affect the child's behaviour and learning and the likely effects should be recognised. Where children may have a fit in the group it is important to reassure staff by doing a thorough risk assessment and gaining confidence in how it will be handled.

## Assessing the child's needs

Many youngsters with cerebral palsy have odd sleep patterns that can affect their readiness to learn. They will be frustrated by their disability and may be angry. Many children, even those with average or above average ability, will have difficulty with speaking, reading, drawing and mathematics. When the children are young it can be difficult to know whether the learning difficulty is because of ability or because of the barriers. One useful way to assess a child's needs is to spend time observing him in different situations. Watch the eyes and watch for signs of anticipation. Does he laugh at adult-to-adult humour? Does she get angry with herself when she can't complete her task? These signs will help you to gauge the level of ability.

Each child is an individual but most children will benefit from the early learning experiences provided. They will enjoy the chance to experience messy play and to be part of a larger group. Most pre-school toys will have additional uses to stimulate listening or speech. Toys that react to voice are often particularly useful, as are cause and effect toys that react to touch. Toys that have interesting smells or textures are useful and can help staff to

develop an understanding of the child's range of expressions of pleasure and dislike!

## Supporting parents

In most cases the parents have already become experts on the way cp affects their child but in some cases, where the child is more mildly affected, the parents may only suspect that there are difficulties and staff may have to help them to get a diagnosis. If parents suspect that their child might have cp they should discuss it with their GP and may find it helpful to contact a local group.

Where the child has already been receiving support, parents and therapists or other carers can give a great deal of information before the child joins the group. It is vital that staff other than the child's support assistant become confident in handling, positioning and communicating with the child. A child may visit the group without this happening, a child may be made welcome, but for the child to be included everyone has to feel confident.

Lindsay Brewis, Lead adviser, Education, Scope.

Scope provides support for children with cerebral palsy and related disabilities, their parents and carers. There is a free and confidential Helpline that pre-school staff, as well as parents, can ring for information or to be put in touch with local services. The number is 0808 800 3333.

**Scope**
6 Market Road, London N7 9PW
www.scope.org.uk/

# Communication
## delay

By the time a child is three, they should have mastered all the skills necessary to communicate with the adults and children in their environment. However, studies show that approximately seven per cent of all children in the UK do not develop those skills.

## What is a communication problem?

Early years workers are likely to come across children with varying degrees of impairment in communication. Broadly speaking, a speech and language impairment means that a child may have difficulty in:

■ how they say their sounds;

■ how much they understand what you say;

■ how much they can say, that is the size of their vocabulary, how many words they can string together to form a sentence.

Types of impairment are:

■ Specific language delay/disorder (differential diagnoses will be discussed later)

■ Phonological delay/disorder

■ Phonetic delay/disorder

■ Developmental dyspraxia

The term 'impairment' includes children who have a delay or disorder. If a child has a delay, we would expect her speech and language to be similar to a child of a younger age - that means that the child is acquiring skills at a slower rate. A 'disorder' exists where skills are not being acquired within the correct/known developmental sequence. Speech and language development is different from the sequential norm.

## Prevalence and causes

Speech and language impairments occur more frequently in boys than girls. It is not always clear why a child has a speech and language impairment. He may be born with it, or could have acquired a speech and language difficulty. Apart from this, the causes aren't clear-cut. A distinction should be made between innate and environmental causes. There are, however, some at risk factors to look out for such as:

■ Family history of speech delay/disorder;

■ Traumatic pregnancy and/or birth;

■ Recurrent ear infections/glue ear;

■ Sensory deprivation;

■ Feeding/swallowing problems;

■ Emotionally deprived/unstable environment;

■ Limited exposure to good models of language at critical points of language development.

## How speech and language impairment manifests itself

A speech or language impairment can affect a child in three ways:

■ behavioural;

■ educational;

■ emotional.

Behaviourally, children with speech and language impairment can be withdrawn and quiet within the class environment or, alternatively, extremely active with poor concentration. They often have difficulty following adult-directed activities, for instance story time, and they tend to respond poorly to verbal instructions. There are children who remain confident speakers in spite of their difficulties; these are generally more outgoing by nature.

These children may display a number of educational characteristics:

■ Make limited contributions to activities that require verbal skills, such as telling a story and during show and tell sessions;

■ Have poor listening skills - instructions need to be repeated a number of times before they are able to carry them out, or they are easily distracted by noises in the classroom;

■ Mispronounce words;

■ They compare well with others on non-verbal tasks;

...mount

...d range
...lary;

- Have difficulty in acquiring new words;

- Find it difficult to find appropriate words to express themselves;

- They mainly use simplified sentences, single words or sounds;

- They put words in the incorrect word order;

- Have difficulty in understanding abstract concepts such as emotions and time;

- Make consistent/inconsistent substitutions of sounds.

The emotional effects could be:

- Have difficulty when playing with their peer group;

- Get frustrated which results in temper tantrums when they can't make their needs known or when they are misunderstood;

- Poor self-esteem;

- Poor integration into their peer group.

## The practitioner's role

If you suspect that a child has a speech and language impairment, the parents or carers must be informed. They, in turn, should tell their GP, health visitor or local child development clinic and ask for a referral to a speech and language therapist.

The child will need an assessment so recommendations on therapy can be made. Therapy can be given on an individual or group basis.

Liaison between the therapist and the pre-school is essential in addressing the child as a whole.

## In the classroom

- Create a good listening environment by using soft furnishings to absorb sound.

- Keep comments short.

- Use as many senses as possible to aid in learning.

- Have a variety of activities available for the child who has poor attention control.

- Vary activities that are challenging, for example listening to a story, with fun and more active types of activities such as painting, outside play or musical chairs.

- Physical contact such as sitting in a worker's lap, can be a great help for children who struggle with attention control and listening.

- Use lots of animation at story time, and rather tell the story in short sentences than reading it word for word.

- Music is a powerful tool in gaining children's attention and stimulating listening and language skills by action songs, for example.

- Using a musical tone of voice can also help.

- Do not make the child talk; instead, follow their focus of attention and comment on what they're doing. The likely response is that the child will naturally want to tell you about his/her interests.

- Regular discussions with parents or carers are helpful when it comes to activities that involve talking within the group. Find out what the child's or family's interests are and when there's a special occasion in the child's life.

- Repeat the child's utterances back to him and model the correct form to him.

- Do not put the child in the spotlight, such as in show and tell activities.

- Avoid asking 'testing questions' like 'What colour is this?' or 'What is this?'. Children with a language impairment feel tested and will naturally withdraw. When you find yourself wanting to ask a testing question, use that moment to *tell* the child what the answer would have been - 'It's a blue truck'.

Reserve time, even just a few moments per day, in a quiet and relaxed environment where you can spend quality time with the child and focus solely on *playing* with him.

## Relationship with parents

A trusting relationship between parents and practitioners is invaluable. Parents are useful sources of information, to help us see and address the child's needs as best we can, taking all aspects of child development into consideration. Specific times need to be set aside to meet with parents. As children with speech and language impairment often struggle with generalisation of concepts, words and skills learned, parents need to reinforce activities at home. Speech and language impairment influences many other areas, social interaction and behaviour and parents frequently need some practical advice on how to help their child at home. Strategies are often put into place in the pre-school that can be successfully applied in the home environment.

Tania Crampton-Hayward, senior paediatric speech and language threrapist at The Speech, Language and Hearing Centre, Christopher Place, London.

### Where to go for help

- Royal College of Speech and Language Therapists, 2-3 White Hart Yard, London SE1 1NX. Tel: 020 7378 1200. Email: info@rcslt.org

- Afasic, 2nd floor, 50-52 Great Sutton Street, London EC1V ODJ. Tel: 020 7490 9410 Helpline (Mon-Fri 11am-2pm Tel: 0845 355 5577) Afasic is the UK charity representing children and young adults with communication impairments.

- The Association of Speech and Language Therapists (ASLTIP), Coleheath Bottom, Speen, Princes Risborough, Bucks HP27 0S2 Tel: 0870 241 3357

- The Speech, Language and Hearing Centre, 1-5 Christopher Place, Chalton Street, London NW1 1JF. Tel: 020 7383 3834. Email: info@speech-lang.org.uk

- Your local education authority

# Stammering
## in young children

Speech is a skill which develops rapidly during a child's first two years as he learns to make meaningful sounds and words. We often take for granted that a child will learn to talk easily and freely but, like learning to walk, there will be bumps, stoppages and starts, before children learn to co-ordinate all the necessary skills and talk smoothly.

Although all children repeat words and phrases, pause between words with ums and ers, and often hesitate, some children will stammer and have more difficulty than others in learning to talk smoothly. There has been a commonly held belief that young children who stammer simply grow out of the problem if it is ignored. However, stammering is a complex problem and parents often wonder if the stammer will get worse, whether they should do something, and if so, what help they should seek.

## What is known about stammering?

Five per cent of all children under five stammer and just over one per cent of school age children. Stammering occurs in all cultures and social groups and affects four times more boys than girls (therefore this text uses 'he' instead of 'she'). It most commonly begins between the ages of two and five years old - the average age of onset is 32 months. Fortunately, most of these children will not continue to stammer into school age, but around two in five are likely to continue to stammer unless they receive help early from a speech and language therapist.

It is not known why young children begin to stammer but it is recognised that a combination of factors is involved. In about 60 per cent of cases, there is a family history of stammering, or other speech and language problems in one or more relatives. However, other factors can affect a child's ability to speak fluently, including their language and motor skills, environmental, social, emotional, and psychological factors.

## How will you know if a child is stammering?

If you look after a child who is stammering there are several things which you may notice:

■ that the child's speech does not seem to flow smoothly - it may sound tense and jerky;

■ the child is putting extra effort into saying his words;

■ the child is aware that he is finding talking difficult or shows signs of being frustrated;

■ that the child gives up talking half way through a sentence or a story.

Or you may hear the child do one or more of the following things:

■ repeat parts of words and whole words; for example 'Ca-ca-ca-can I have a drink?' or 'I-I-I-I want a story';

■ lengthen sounds; for example, 'He is sssssssitting on the chair';

■ block - this is where the child knows what he wants to say but gets stuck on a particular word; for example 'Where's . . . . . . . . daddy gone?'

Stammering varies a great deal from child to child so you may hear some or all of these things when the child is talking.

One of the features of early stammering is that it tends to come and go. Children can often have days, weeks or months when their speech seems to flow easily and smoothly and the stammer seems to have disappeared, and other times when the stammering is more noticeable and the child finds talking difficult again. Even within one day you may notice that a child's stammering varies:

- it may be more obvious when he is feeling tired, unwell, excited, or anxious;

- it may change depending on who he is talking to, for example other children, adults, carers or strangers;

- or according to the situation, for example if it is noisy, quiet, rushed or relaxed.

## What should you do?

Because you are with the child regularly you hear him speak at different times of the day and in different situations, for example when he is playing alone or in a group, first thing in the morning or when he is more awake, so you are in an ideal position to notice if a child is stammering or finds talking difficult.

If you think a child you look after is stammering the first thing to do is to discuss this with his parents or carers. If stammering is identified and treated early enough, therapy is effective and can help the child overcome the stammering. Therefore if a parent/carer is concerned in any way it is important that they do not delay in asking for a referral to their local NHS speech and language therapy (SLT) service either through their health visitor or GP, or directly, by contacting the SLT department.

## Practical ways of helping

There are many things you can do to help a child who stammers talk more easily.

- Listen and respond to what the child wants to say not how he says it.

- Don't look away from the child when he stammers.

## 'If stammering is identified and treated early enough, therapy is effective and can help the child overcome the stammering.'

- Be patient and allow the child time to complete his thoughts and to speak rather than finishing the child's sentences or interrupting him.

- Reduce the number of questions you ask, and make sure you give the child time to answer one before asking another.

- Slow down your own rate of speech slightly - this is more helpful than asking the child to slow down or to stop and start again. Slowing down helps the child feel less rushed when they talk.

- Wait a second or so before responding to a child's comments or questions - pausing like this helps children feel less hurried when it is their turn to talk and gives them time before answering.

- Praise and encourage the child for what he does well. This helps build confidence.

- Treat a child who stammers in the same way as other children regarding their behaviour - discipline should be appropriate and consistent.

Children who stammer respond well to a less hurried lifestyle and in a structured environment and a routine.

If the child needs to tell you something, give him your full attention. If you are doing something else at the time, explain why you cannot stop, but give him your full attention later.

## Where to go for more help

If you suspect a child you look after is stammering, it is important that his parents or carers seek professional help from a speech and language therapist (SLT) as soon as they become concerned - preferably from an SLT who specialises in stammering. Stammering can be prevented from developing if it is treated early enough.

Parents and professionals can contact the British Stammering Association's Information and Counselling Service to receive a free information pack, details of their local NHS speech and language therapist service and whom to contact to make a referral.

Copies of the leaflets *Does Your Young Child Stammer?* and *Stammering in the Under Fives - Information for Professionals* are available free to all early years settings from the BSA.

Other useful books include *Helping Children Cope with Stammering* by Trudy Stewart and Jackie Turnbull and *Stuttering and Your Child: Questions and Answers* from the Stuttering Foundation of America.

Elaine Christie is a specialist speech and language therapist working in private practice in London and Kent. Before that she managed an early identification project at the British Stammering Association.

You can contact
The British Stammering
Association on
0845 603 2001
(information and
counselling service, local
rate call) or write to
them at:
British Stammering
Association, 15 Old Ford
Road, London E2 9PJ.
Main office number:

**0208 983 1003**

# Including **the child**
## with Down's syndrome

The human body is made up of cells. Each cell is like a tiny factory, which makes the materials needed for growth and maintenance of the body. Contained within each cell is a set of 46 chromosomes (23 pairs), half of which come from the person's mother and half from the father. The chromosomes carry the genes that are inherited from a person's parents.

## What is Down's syndrome?

Down's syndrome is a condition that occurs at or around the time a baby is conceived. Most people with Down's syndrome have an extra copy of chromosome 21 in every cell, making 47 in all. It is not yet known what causes this to happen. However, it is something that occurs in all races and all social classes. It is known that the chance of having a baby with Down's syndrome is higher in older mothers, although, because more babies overall are born to mothers in the 25- to 30-year-old age group, the majority of babies with Down's syndrome are born to 25- to 30-year-old women. We do know that, in the vast majority of cases, Down's syndrome is not passed down from generation to generation.

The presence of the extra chromosome has the effect of disrupting the growth and development of the baby. Quite how much effect the extra chromosome has varies from person to person, although all people who have Down's syndrome have a certain degree of learning disability.

People with Down's syndrome are as different from each other as any other unrelated members of the population.

Like the rest of us, they get all their genes from their parents, so they look and act much more like members of their family than someone else with Down's syndrome. Their abilities and skills, strengths and weaknesses are just as variable as they are amongst the rest of us.

It is important not to make generalisations about people with Down's syndrome, but to look at each person as an individual.

## How common is Down's syndrome?

In every 1,000 live births, one baby will be born with Down's syndrome. That is about 600 babies every year in the UK.

## Diagnosis

In most cases, it becomes clear quite soon after birth that the baby has Down's syndrome. Doctors and midwives are usually alerted by certain signs that are more common among babies with Down's syndrome than among other babies. For example, if doctors detect a heart disorder it may alert them to the possibility of Down's syndrome because about 40 per cent of babies with Down's syndrome also have a heart problem. Diagnosis can be confirmed by a blood test to analyse the chromosomes.

It is important to stress that it is not possible to tell how disabled a child will be at this early stage. The number of physical characteristics of Down's syndrome a child has bears no relation to his or her degree of developmental delay.

## Developmental delay

For a variety of reasons, such as poor health and/or hospitalisation at an early age, some young children with Down's syndrome will be more delayed than others. By the time children reach three or four, it may be apparent that they are not as advanced as their ordinary peers. Nowadays, most young children with Down's syndrome will have benefited from an early intervention programme (sometimes known as Portage) designed to help them gain the skills that other children learn naturally. Such programmes can be encouraging to parents who feel they can be actively involved in promoting their child's development. An early intervention worker will help parents to teach their child by breaking down tasks into small manageable steps. In some areas of the country, Portage is available from the age of six months; in others it starts later.

## Speech and language delay

Speech and language difficulties are common in young children with Down's syndrome. Most children will be under the care of a speech and language therapist who will give parents and carers (including early years workers) guidelines on how to encourage the speech and language development of the child according to an individual programme.

## Common health problems

Children's development can be delayed because of health problems that are more common in Down's syndrome.

### Hearing

Many children with Down's syndrome have hearing problems caused by a condition called glue ear, which can be a consequence of repeated upper respiratory infections such as colds, or infected or enlarged adenoids. The fluid in the ear becomes thick like jelly and cannot drain away and hearing is affected. This can happen in all children but it is more frequent in children with Down's syndrome. Glue ear can cause deafness, infection, pain, delayed speech

*'Most parents of a child with Down's syndrome will have become experts on their child's condition and needs. They need to feel that their views and knowledge are being respected and taken into account. Communication is the key to successful inclusion and many potential problems can be avoided by both parties keeping the other informed.'*

development, and temporary behaviour problems. Glue ear can be successfully treated, but early years workers need to be aware that the effects of hearing impairment can be reduced by a few simple steps outlined below:

- Always give the child plenty of time to respond to anything you have said - they will get frustrated if you start saying something new before they have had time to respond to the first thing you said. (This applies to most children with Down's syndrome whether or not they have any degree of hearing loss.)

- Try to face the child when speaking to them.

- Don't shout but speak clearly.

- If the child does not understand, don't just repeat what has been said but try to rephrase it.

- Make sure the child is paying attention before you start speaking.

- Give the child lots of visual clues - signs and gestures - to help them understand what you are saying.

- Keep your hands and any visual aids away from your mouth.

- Don't use exaggerated lip movements.

### Vision problems
Some young children with Down's syndrome need glasses to correct their vision and, just as with other children who wear glasses, you may need to make sure that the child does wear them when necessary.

### Lack of muscle tone
Many babies with Down's syndrome have poor muscle tone and tend to be 'floppy'. In most cases, this improves as the child grows. However, it can contribute to delay in learning how to run, skip, throw and catch (gross motor skills) and affect the development of skills such as writing (fine motor development). Most children will master these skills eventually, but may take longer than their peers to do so. Many young children with Down's syndrome will have regular physiotherapy sessions either at home or at a child development centre. These sessions are designed to give parents exercises to do with their children to help them achieve particular skills.

### Where to go for help
Your Local Education Authority's Special Education Department should be able to provide advice and support to staff who are involved in including a child with Down's syndrome in a pre-school setting.

The Down's Syndrome Association has an information service and also a number of advisers it can call on for specific information about such things as speech therapy, medical and behaviour problems. Lists of the DSA's leaflets and recommended reading are available to anyone who sends in a stamped addressed envelope to:

The Down's Syndrome Association, 155 Mitcham Road, Tooting, London SW17 9PG. Telephone: 0208 682 4001.

E-mail: info@downs-syndrome.org.uk

Website address: www.downs-syndrome.org.uk

### Monitoring development
The developmental progress of children with Down's syndrome will usually be monitored by staff at the local child development centre. In the early years, parents are often offered extra support by a specialist health visitor or a social worker who is able to keep them informed of facilities for children with special needs in the area.

### How to cope with questions about difference
Pre-school children in general tend to accept differences in colour, behaviour and so on much more readily than older children might. Most of the time, if children in a group ask questions about a child being different, it will be enough to point out that we are all different - 'You have blonde hair but Jessica has black hair'. The Down's Syndrome Association (see box) has a list of recommended reading books for children which deal with issues of difference.

### Relationships with parents/carers
Most parents of a child with Down's syndrome will have become experts on their child's condition and needs. They need to feel that their views and knowledge are being respected and taken into account. Communication is the key to successful inclusion and many potential problems can be avoided by both parties keeping the other informed. It may be helpful to remember that a child with Down's syndrome is a child first and foremost and that his or her condition is secondary.

Sarah Rutter, Information Manager, The Down's Syndrome Association.

# Understanding **dyslexia**

In the past, it was thought children could only be diagnosed as dyslexic from the age of six. It is now evident that there are many signs well before school age. Parents and pre-school carers and educators are in the strongest position to recognise those signs, and to provide the right activities to help.

The word 'dyslexia' was originally coined from the Greek and, taken literally, means 'difficulty with words'. The old way of describing it was 'word blindness' – an inability to read letters and numbers in the right order. However, that's far from the whole picture.

Dyslexia is best described as a combination of abilities and difficulties which affect the learning process in one or more of reading, spelling, writing and sometimes numeracy.

Accompanying weaknesses may be identified in areas of speed of processing, short-term memory, sequencing, auditory and/or visual perception, spoken language and motor skills.

Some children have outstanding creative skills, others have strong oral skills. While not every dyslexic child will be outstandingly talented, all have their own strengths.

Dyslexia occurs despite normal intellectual ability and conventional teaching. It is independent of socio-economic or language background.

Britain has two million severely dyslexic individuals, equivalent to four per cent of the population. This figure includes around 375,000 schoolchildren. A further three million people have dyslexia in its mild or moderate forms.

This means that it affects about ten per cent of the population, either directly or indirectly. Put another way, 20 per cent of all children with special educational needs will be dyslexic. It is vital that such children's abilities and difficulties are identified as early as possible and that the right teaching provision is put in place.

## Early signs

A child's behaviour may be an early indicator of learning differences. It can range from diffidence and a lack of self-esteem to the other extreme – being cocky and acting the class clown.

In addition, a pre-school child who is potentially dyslexic may:

- Know colours but confuse them – for example saying 'black' instead of 'brown'

- Have an early lisp

- Struggle to remember the label for known objects – for example table, chair

- Confuse directional words like up/down, in/out

- Find it hard to learn nursery rhymes or even rhyming words

- Have a problem with sequences – for example coloured beads – and later with things like days of the week or numbers

## Possible causes

Experts don't always agree on where the exact cause of dyslexia lies. Researchers at Sheffield University have found that the cerebellum area of the brain, which controls movement – anything from riding a bicycle to threading a needle, doesn't function as well as it should in dyslexic people.

Dr John Stein of Oxford University points out that dyslexics often have difficulties with precise movements – and the eye movements needed for reading are extraordinarily precise. His research indicates that dyslexic people have a problem measuring the timing of messages from both the eyes and the ears.

Most researchers into causes of dyslexia are looking at the area of the brain affecting language. Most dyslexic people, even when good readers, have continuing difficulties with phonological awareness – recognising sounds and analysing small parts of speech. Many experience some difficulties with speaking words – thinking of the right word for an object, muddling words, for example by saying par cark instead of car park or rapid naming, for example quickly saying ten animals beginning with 's'.

## Supporting the dyslexic child

These activities will benefit the whole pre-school group not just those children who may be dyslexic.

- Say nursery rhymes together

- Finger play

*'Dyslexia is best described as a combination of abilities and difficulties which affect the learning process in one or more of reading, spelling, writing and sometimes numeracy.'*

- Read poetry to children, especially amusing or nonsense verse. Try making up jingles or limericks.

- Mime a particular nursery rhyme or incident and encourage the children to guess the rhyme. They can then choose something to rhyme in return.

- Use drama

- Provide pictures to talk about, using prepositions in discussion: 'Is the man in the blue hat in front of or behind the lady?'

- Hunt the thimble – is it inside or under the pot?

- Play 'Simon says' – starting with simple instructions but gradually making them more difficult – for example 'Simon says touch your ear and your nose then clap your hands'

- Other useful games to play include 'Follow my leader' and the 'Hokey-cokey'

- Board games like snakes and ladders, ludo and bingo help develop turn-taking

- There are some good puzzle books in bookshops and stationers. Joining dots, mazes and simple picture crosswords can all be useful

- Tap a simple rhythm for the child to repeat. Clap words of one syllable before moving on to two-syllable words, then more. Say the words as you clap them – for example tel – e – vi – sion. Also use the child's name for this activity. Can he or she say how many beats the word has?

- Use songs involving memory and sequencing – for example 'Old Macdonald had a farm'

- 'I went to market and I bought...' – start with a particular group of things, for example fruit and veg, because it is easier to remember related things. Later, shop for random things – or things where each item should have the same letter – for example pancakes, pens, peanuts, potatoes

- Say a group of words with a 'stranger' in it – for example 'cat', 'dog', 'apple', 'fox'. The child tells you or draws a picture of the stranger. Ask why it is different. This game can also be played with rhyming words, for example 'cat', 'bat', 'fox', 'hat'. Which word didn't rhyme?

## Relationships with parents

For some parents, it may be a relief that someone else has picked up on their child's difficulties. They may have noticed problems but not voiced them or they may have attempted to express their feelings and met with comments like 'Don't worry. Don't expect too much. He will catch up.' At worst, the parent may have been labelled fussy, pushy or overanxious.

Building a strong partnership with parents is vital. Bear in mind that dyslexic difficulties can be extremely sensitive and it is important to broach the subject with sympathy and tact. A mother, in particular, is often perceptive about her own child. Her comments should always be listened to, and her concerns taken seriously.

Remember to emphasise the positive aspects of dyslexia and that it is common. Today, dyslexia is viewed as a combination of abilities as well as difficulties. Dyslexic people may have good problem-solving skills, enhanced creativity and excel in the arts, design, architecture and computing. Stress that, with the right intervention and support at this early stage in the child's education, there is no reason why he or she should not thrive.

## Where to get help

During regular pre-school development checks, a doctor or health visitor may see children with an uneven development profile, indicating weaker areas which need attention from a speech or language therapist and/or an occupational therapist to look at fine motor co-ordination problems, and/or a paediatric physiotherapist for gross motor problems.

## Further support, information and advice is available from:

The British Dyslexia Association
98 London Road
Reading
RG1 5AU
Tel: 0118 966 2677 (admin)
Helpline: 0118 966 8271
Monday to Friday, 10am–12.45pm, 2–4.45pm
email: info@dyslexiahelp-bda.demon.co.uk
www.bda-dyslexia.org.uk

The BDA publishes *Catch 'em Young*, a guide for pre-school educators, for £7.50 including postage and packing. Cheques should be made payable to the BDA, and sent to the above address.

It is helpful if information from all these sources, along with parents' and pre-school educators' comments, are made available to the headteacher when the child enters his first school. The valuable observations and record-keeping of parents and early years educators can prevent the situation where it takes several years for a child to be identified as dyslexic, by which time failure and consequent behavioural problems may well be all too apparent.

Juliet England, British Dyslexia Association.

# Understanding
attention deficit/
hyperactivity disorder

Research suggests that attention deficit/hyperactivity disorder or AD/HD is genetic and bio-neurological in origin, but there are still those who claim it is an excuse for parents and teachers who cannot cope with normal, albeit challenging, children. The use of medication to treat AD/HD is also controversial: is it a mind-altering drug used to control children for our own convenience or an effective treatment for a neurological impairment?

Having reviewed the research on AD/HD, the British College of Psychiatrists stated, in their publication *FOCUS: On the Use of*

> *'Because the prognosis for many children with AD/HD is not good - many of them go on to have social, vocational and relationship problems - early identification is critically important.'*

*Stimulants in Children with AD/HD*, that we should see the disorder as a threshold which can be reached by a combination of inherited, social and psychological factors. This helps to explain why there is a high family incidence of AD/HD, affecting five to nine times as many males than females. Estimates of prevalence vary between two and five per cent, but if the same raters, using the same criteria, assess a group of children for AD/HD the number is fairly constant across all ability levels, cultures, and classes.

There are three types of AD/HD:

- children who are predominantly hyperactive and impulsive;

- children who are predominantly inattentive;

- children who have AD/HD combined and are both hyperactive/impulsive *and* inattentive.

## Common characteristics

Parents and teachers typically describe the first and last of these two groups in the following way: driven by a motor, restless, fidgety, volatile, attention seeking, unable to sit still, unable to listen, distractible, quickly bored, demanding, bossy, accident prone, 'in your face' and highly impulsive - acting first and thinking second. The children usually have problems with waiting and turn-taking - in conversation, games and queues - and find it almost impossible to raise a hand rather than shouting out. The AD/HD toddler can seem unkind: pushing another child out of the way, snatching a preferred toy and sometimes acting aggressively. Attempts to control the child frequently result in a temper tantrum.

Conversely, children who have the inattentive version of AD/HD are often dreamy, under-active, ambivalent children who are easily overlooked by their peers and at risk for learning difficulties. More girls than boys fall into this category, which affects less children than the other forms of AD/HD.

I will focus on the more common forms of AD/HD (hyperactive/impulsive and combined). At a psychological level, the core problem for these children is poor self-control. Areas of the pre-frontal lobes - the part of the brain that deals with self-management - are under active and, as a result, it is hard for the children to control their activity level, behaviour and mood. These problematic behaviours have an early onset and are persistent over time and across settings. However, children with AD/HD can have distinctly good and bad days and nearly always behave well in a clinic where they enjoy the novelty and

attention. This raises an important fact about AD/HD: these children do not have problems concentrating on favoured activities. In fact the opposite is true: because it takes self-control to stop doing something you enjoy it can be much harder for a child with AD/HD to stop watching TV or playing with his video than it is for his non-AD/HD sibling or classmate.

## Diagnosing AD/HD

Diagnosing AD/HD is exceptionally difficult for several reasons. Firstly, many other disorders present with similar or overlapping symptoms, and more than half of the children with AD/HD have other areas of difficulty. Secondly, AD/HD is not a categorical condition, such as a broken leg which is either broken or not broken, but a continuum disorder where the cut-off point is not always clear. Thirdly, environmental factors, such as a disruption in attachment, can sometimes cloud the issue. Lastly, there is no test for AD/HD: diagnosis depends upon clinical judgement, which is why multi-agency assessment is all important.

Because the prognosis for many children with AD/HD is not good - many of them go on to have social, vocational and relationship problems - early identification is critically important.

## Supporting children with AD/HD

The recent and highly important Multi-Modal Treatment of Attention Deficit/Hyperactivity Disorder study, conducted by the American National Institute of Mental Health, showed that stimulant medication is the most effective way of managing the core AD/HD symptoms (although other, associated behaviours, also require behaviour management), but medication is not recommended for children under the age of six, and many parents understandably do not want to go down this route. It is hard work to support a child with AD/HD without medication, but it can be done! If you suspect you have a child with AD/HD in your pre-school group or class, here are some suggestions.

Firstly, discuss the problems with the child's parent/s or caregivers (in practise usually the mother). Be careful not to use negative language such as 'naughty' or 'bad' that will make the mother feel she is being judged as a poor parent. Start off with positives, describing the child as lively rather than hyperactive, full of enthusiasm rather than impulsive. Never discuss the child while he is present, in front of other parents or in a public place such as the playground.

Before you see the mother, write out a list of problems and then use the 'Three basket' method. In the first basket put the problems that are harmful or illegal: running out of the playground or hurting other children. In the second basket put the problems that seriously annoy you such as constant shouting. In the third basket put everything else. Now accept that you can only tackle one or two problems at a time, choose the problems from the first basket, and only discuss these problems with the mother. This will counter feelings of helplessness, give you a realistic chance of success and the confidence to tackle new targets.

Make a plan. The target must be realistic or both you and the child will fail. It must also be clear and simple so that the child understands exactly what you mean. For example, if you ask a child to be 'kind' he will argue relentlessly when you say he has not been kind. Be explicit: being kind involves no biting, thumping, pinching or hitting. Use circle time to discuss what we mean by kindness, and at the start of each day give every child five smiley faces. If they are unkind they lose a face: if they are extra kind or helpful to another child they can win a face back. At the end of the day, children with three faces have a certificate to take home.

Research has shown that this method, which is called 'response cost', is particularly effective with children who have AD/HD. These children need immediate rewards, and are better if they start with the reward than if they work towards it. It also means that a child can win back all they have lost, and this is particularly important for children with AD/HD as they give up easily.

In addition to this specific plan, here are some other strategies which research shows are effective:

■ Try to have a calm, organised classroom with an established daily routine. Warn the child well ahead of any changes, such as a new helper, and prepare the child for changes of activity: 'We'll be packing up in ten minutes, five minutes - I'll put the cooker timer on so that you can see how much time you have left'.

■ Try to ignore minor naughtiness and be sure to praise the child - even for something small - at least three times each day. Be quick and generous with praise.

■ When a child is naughty, make sure he knows you like him but not his behaviour.

■ Make sure the other children know you like the child. Social rejection is a major problem for children with AD/HD, and we know that it has an early onset and is slow to turn around. It is also true that children who are popular with their teacher are more likely to be popular with their peers.

■ Never resort to anger, ridicule or sarcasm. This will inflame the situation and have a lasting effect on the child.

■ Never get involved in an argument: this is highly rewarding to children with AD/HD. Simply state, in a relaxed, calm voice: 'You know the rule, it's your choice' and then remove your attention. It is difficult to do, but effective!

■ When faced with a melt-down tantrum give the child an opportunity to calm down and save face by saying: 'OK, you can play for another five minutes'. After five minutes the child will often back down and you can then discuss the matter. This has been found to be much more effective and less disruptive than trying to insist on immediate compliance.

■ Avoid confrontation by giving the child choices. For example, when he refuses to draw a picture ask: 'Do you want to draw with felt-tips or crayons?', or 'Do you want to finish your picture before drink time or after?'

■ Try to make eye contact with the child when you are talking to him.

■ Have a home/school diary so that you are in constant touch with the parents.

■ Adopt a whole-school approach and support one another.

Remember that if you can help a child with AD/HD in these formative years you are significantly improving his chances of a happy, successful life. If the problems prove intractable, this in itself is valuable evidence that should be passed on to the school educational psychologist or medical officer.

## References

Multi-Modal Treatment of Attention Deficit/Hyperactivity Disorder (MTA study) Numerous papers have been published about this study. Details can be found on the following website: www.devdis.com

Royal College of Psychiatrists' Research Unit, 1999, *FOCUS on the Use of Stimulants in Children with AD/HD*

Jenny Lyon, specialist educational psychologist.

## Resources

Information about AD/HD and other developmental disorders, contacts for family support groups, recommended books, videos and training can all be found on the following website: www.devdis.com. Jenny Lyon can answer questions on the website forum or contact International Psychology Services (IPS), 17 High Street, Hurstpierpoint, West Sussex BN6 9TT.

Please note that 'he' rather than 'she/he' is used throughout as the majority of children with AD/HD are male.

# Dyspraxia or developmental coordination disorder (DCD)

**Until ten to fifteen years ago the term dyspraxia, meaning a deficit in movement planning, hadn't been heard of in the UK. Children with motor coordination difficulties would probably have just been thought of as clumsy.**

Dyspraxia - also known as developmental coordination disorder or DCD - is about ten years behind in terms of its acknowledgement and research in comparison to dyslexia. It is part of a spectrum of specific learning difficulties along with AD/HD (attention deficit/ hyperactivity disorder), Asperger's syndrome and dyslexia. It affects between four and six per cent of the population and about three times as many boys as girls.

## What causes DCD?
There has been little research completed looking at the causes of developmental coordination disorder. There are both environmental and genetic factors at play. This means that often someone else in the family may have had dyslexia or other learning difficulties but when they were growing up they may not have been recognised.

## Is the incidence of DCD on the increase?
More children are now being identified as having dyspraxia and this may be due to an increase in the condition because of different parenting styles today.

## How have parenting styles changed?
The 'Back to sleep' campaign now encourages parents to place babies on their back for the majority of the time. In the past, they would have put babies to sleep in prams or cots during the day and placed them prone as well as on their backs.

Nowadays, most babies are usually either in a car seat, which is carried in and out from the car, and placed on the floor, or in a pushchair. In both cases the child is supine (on the back) rather than in a prone (on the front) position. Children are not placed on a baby mat on the floor as often as they used to for fear of it being dirty. The use of playpens has also been limited as they are now seen as trapping the baby, rather than allowing them to explore their environment safely.

For most babies, these changes won't have a long-term affect. However, for the low - toned, floppy child, the opportunity to gain greater head and shoulder control and hip stability is essential for future development. The floppy baby is also likely to cry when placed prone, as he is not able to lift his head for any length of time. This, combined with changes in parenting styles, may be the reason why there is a growing incidence of non-crawlers as well as more cases of DCD being identified.

The prone position is important as it allows the child to strengthen the neck muscles, do push-ups (ready for crawling) and learn to reach for toys (helping hand- eye coordination and bilateral integration).

The child with DCD may also walk later and for this reason may be put in a baby walker. Yet the child with DCD often has poor hip stability and the modern baby walker tends to make them sit down rather than use it as a support. He then moves around not just in a forward direction but also sideways like a crab! The older style walker with bricks in it made the child stand up to hold on to the bar in a good walking style.

Children with DCD also often have sequencing and rhythm problems that

*'More children are now being identified as having dyspraxia and this may be due to an increase in the condition because of different parenting styles today.'*

affect them in games and with activities like writing and mathematics. Early games played at home such as singing nursery rhymes, catching and throwing balls are less common as children turn to television and video for entertainment, even at a young age.

Fewer children are eating together with families at mealtimes and this means that they are not getting the chance to practise key skills such as using cutlery (helps bilateral integration skills - a pre-cursor for writing) and sitting at the table and taking turns (helping, listening and social skills).

Children's diets have also changed. Today we eat more processed foods and less fish regularly. There is growing evidence that fatty acid supplements such as cod liver oil or Eye-Q (available over the counter at chemists) are especially helpful because it is thought that some children with dyspraxia have problems metabolising certain fatty acids needed for brain and eye activity.

## How would you recognise a child that may have dyspraxia?

■ Late motor milestones - this means that the child may have been later sitting, crawling, walking or talking. Some children may not have crawled at all.

■ Balance problems – the child may be unreasonably afraid or conversely unaware of danger in precarious situations. Climbing on a climbing frame or along a wall or walking downstairs may make the child very nervous. The child may also be unstable if not sat properly in a chair with their feet on the floor.

■ Poor bilateral integration – the child may find it difficult to coordinate both sides of the body. This may make using a knife and fork or handwriting harder to do.

■ He may seem to run in a rather ungainly manner, may need to use his arms to help balance, and find that stopping is quite hard to do. Catching and throwing a ball may be harder to do as well as being able to stand on one leg, skip or jump.

■ Younger children often find a bicycle is harder to pedal.

## Fine motor skills

■ Immature grasp and poor dexterity – There may be difficulty holding and manipulating small objects, for example doing up buttons, holding and using a pencil, using scissors and playing with jigsaws.

■ Poorly established dominance – the child may not seem to be clearly right- or left-handed. He may use whichever hand is nearer to reach.

■ The child may have poor pencil control, and find drawing and colouring in harder to do than his peers.

## Learning difficulties

The child with DCD may experience difficulties with:

■ Letter and shape recognition

■ Writing - their writing may vary in size and quality from the top of the page to the bottom. The letters may go above and below lines on the page. (Even at the age of seven or eight the child may still have writing that looks more like a four- or five-year-old's.)

■ Counting and recognising numbers

## Language and communication

■ The child may have been slower to acquire clear speech and may still have poor speech which may be less distinct when the child is tired.

■ The child may not join in with other children, playing alongside rather than interacting with them.

■ He may appear at times not to be listening.

## Behaviour and emotion

■ Distractible- the child may appear to be distractible but this may be because of his inability to balance on a chair or filter out unwanted sounds, movement or a visually busy environment.

■ Frustration – this usually presents for the younger child with behaviour which is better in school than at home. The child may have tantrums even as he gets older, especially at home.

## So what can be done?

If you suspect that a child may have dyspraxia, early recognition and prevention is better than intervention. Therapy will help some children if their symptoms are more severe but plenty of play experiences to build up muscle control are important. Some schools even provide programmes to promote motor development. For the younger child, the best advice is to encourage big play, such as setting up obstacle courses, playing on the floor and swimming. Give them a big paintbrush and a bucket of

## Where can you go for help?

The parents' first port of call should be their GP or health visitor.

The Dyscovery Centre assesses and treats children with dyspraxia and supports their families but can also help with information for teachers. The centre provides awareness days and has a one-stop shop for toys and equipment.

The Dyscovery Centre
4a Church Road
Whitchurch
Cardiff
Tel: 02920 628222
Website: www.dyscovery.co.uk

The Dyspraxia Foundation is a national charity promoting the awareness and understanding of dyspraxia. It publishes information, organises conferences and has local groups across the UK.

The Dyspraxia Foundation
8 West Alley
Hitchin
Hertfordshire SG5 1EG
Tel: 01462 454986
Website:
www.emmbrook.demon.co.uk/dysprax/homepage.htm

water and let them 'paint' the walls or fence outside.

Make sure the child has their basic building block skills in place before moving onto more complicated work. The child with DCD often seems younger and just needs a bit of extra time to learn new skills.

They should see their GP or health visitor who could refer them on to a children's centre for a full assessment.

For parents, one of the most important things is to be kept informed of what help and support their child is receiving in your setting and who they should liaise with (SENCO or class teacher) and where they can get further advice through the education authority and local support groups.

Dr Amanda Kirby, Medical Director, The Dyscovery Centre, Cardiff.

# *Observation* **record**

| Child's name | | Date | |
|---|---|---|---|

**Focus/purpose of observation**



**Details of observation/behaviours, learning difficulties observed**



**Evaluation/suggestions**



**Signed** _____

# *Expression* **of concern**

**Name** [                    ]    **Date of birth** [        ]

**What difficulties are evident?**



**What strategies have been tried in response to these needs?**



**Which outside agencies have been consulted/with what outcome?**



**Signed** _____

# *Individual Education* **Plan**

For: _____     D.O.B: _____

Early Years Action   / Action Plus / Statement of SEN

Period of plan: _____     Date: _____

| **Strengths / interests** | **Learning needs** |
|---|---|
| | |
| **Targets** | **Strategies** |
| | |
| **Resources** | **Monitoring, assessment and success criteria** |
| | |

Agreed by: _____ SENCO

_____ Parent

Date for review:

# *Review* **document**

Name [                    ]    Date [          ]

**Progress made towards targets**

**Effectiveness of strategies/plan**

**Parental support/external agencies**

**New/updated information**

**Future action**

**Present at review**

Signed: _____ SENCO

# Useful addresses

**Action for Leisure**
Warwickshire College, Moreton Morrell, Warwickshire CV35 7PP. Tel: 01926 650195.

**Advisory Centre for Education (ACE)**
Unit 1B, Aberdeen Studios, 22 Highbury Grove, London N5 2DQ. Tel: 0207 354 8321 Freephone helpline: 0808 800 5793 2-5pm weekdays Website: www.ace-ed.org.uk A national advice centre for parents offering information and support about state education in England and Wales for five- to 16-year-olds.

**Afasic**
2nd floor, 50-52 Great Sutton Street, London EC1V ODJ. Helpline: 0845 355 5577 The UK charity representing children and young adults with communication impairments.

**Association of Speech and Language Therapists (ASLTIP)**
Coleheath Bottom, Speen, Princes Risborough, Bucks HP27 0S2. Tel: 0870 241 3357

**British Dyslexia Association**
98 London Road, Reading RG1 5AU. Tel: 0118 966 2677 Helpline: 0118 966 8271 Website: www.bda-dyslexia.org.uk

**British Stammering Association**
15 Old Ford Road, London E2 9PJ. Tel: 0208 983 1003

**Centre for Accessible Environments**
Nutmeg House, 60 Gainsford Street, London SE1 2NY. Tel: 0207 357 8182. Information access and design.

**Centre for Studies on Inclusive Education**
Room 2S203 S Block, Frenchay Campus, Coldharbour Lane, Bristol BS16 IQU. Tel: 0117 344 4007

**Contact a Family (CAF)**
209-211 City Road, London EC1V 1JN. Tel: 020 7608 8700 Freephone helpine: 0808 808 3555 Provides support and advice to parents of children with special needs.

**Council for Disabled Children**
8 Wakley Street, London EC1V 7QE. Tel: 020 7843 6061 Email: cdc@ncb.org.uk Website: www.ncb.org.uk/cdc.htm

**DIAL UK (Disablement Information and Advice Lines)**
St Catherines, Tickhill Road, Doncaster DN4 8QN. Supports a network of local disablement information and advice officers. Telephone 01302 310123 to find out who your local officer is.

**Disabled Living Foundation**
380-384 Harrow Road, London W9 2HU. Tel: 0207 289 6111. Helpline: 0845 130 9177

**Down's Syndrome Association**
155 Mithcam Road, Tooting, London SW17 9PG. Tel: 0208 682 4001 Website: www.downs-syndrome.org.uk

**Dyspraxia Foundation**
8 West Alley, Hitchin, Herts SG5 1EG. Tel: 01462 454986 Website: www.emmbrook.demon.co.uk/dysprax/homepage.htm

**The Dyscovery Centre**
4a Church Road, Whitchurch, Cardiff. Tel: 029 2062 8222 The centre assesses and treats children with dyspraxia but can also help with information.

**Home-Start UK,**
2 Salisbury Road, Leicester LE1 7QR. Tel: 0116 233 9955 Website: www.home-start.org.uk

**Kidsactive**
(formerly HAPA), Pryor's Bank, Bishop's Park, London SW6 3LA. Tel: 0207 731 1435 and 020 7736 4443. National charity providing information and training on inclusive play.

**LOOK**
Part of the National Federation of Families with Visually Impaired Children. Queen Alexandra College, 49 Court Oak Road, Harborne, Birmingham B17 9TG. Tel: 0121 428 5038 Website: www.look-uk.org

**MENCAP**
123 Golden Lane, London EC1Y ORT. Tel: 0207 454 0454. Can advise on working with children with learning difficulties.

**National Association for Special Educational Needs (NASEN)**
NASEN House, 4/5 Amber Business Village, Amber Close, Amington, Tamworth B77 4RP. Tel: 01827 311500 Website: www.nasen.org.uk

**National Autistic Society**
393 City Road, London EC1V 1NE. Tel: 0207 903 3599 Helpline: 0207 903 3555

**National Deaf Children's Society**
15 Dufferin Street, London EC1Y 8PD. Tel/Minicom: 0808 800 8880. Can advise on communicating with deaf children.

**National Portage Association**
PO Box 3075, Yeovil, Somerset BA21 3JF. Tel: 01935 471641 Website: www.portage.org.uk

**Parents for Inclusion**
Unit 2, 70 south Lambeth Road, London SW8 IRL. Tel: 0207 735 7735. An organisation set up by parents of disabled children to provide support and advice to parents and to campaign for the inclusion of disabled children in mainstream education.

**Partially Sighted Society**
Queen's Road, Doncaster DN1 2NX. Tel: 01302 323132

**Royal College of Speech and Language Therapists**
2-3 White Hart Yard, London SE1 1NX. Tel: 020 7378 1200

**Royal National Institute for the Blind (RNIB)**
105 Judd Street, London WC1H 9NE. Tel: 0207 388 1266. Can advise on many aspects of play and leisure for visually impaired children.

**Scope**
6 Market Road, London N7 9PW. Provides support for children with cerebral palsy and related disabilities, their parents and carers. Helpline: 0808 800 3333